WALL
STREET
JOURNAL
BOOKS

WINNING
WITH
THE MARKET

DOUGLAS R. SEASE

A WALL STREET JOURNAL BOOK

Published by Simon & Schuster, Inc.

NEW YORK   LONDON   TORONTO   SYDNEY   SINGAPORE

A WALL STREET JOURNAL BOOK
Rockefeller Center
Published by Simon & Schuster, Inc.
1230 Avenue of the Americas
New York, NY 10020

This Wall Street Journal Book Edition 2002

SIMON & SCHUSTER and colophon are registered
trademarks of Simon & Schuster , Inc.

The Wall Street Journal and the Wall Street Journal Book
colophon are trademarks of Dow Jones & Company, Inc.

For information about special discounts for bulk purchases,
please contact Simon & Schuster Special Sales:
1-800-456-6798 or business@simonandschuster.com

Manufactured in the United States of America

10 9 8 7 6 5 4 3 2 1

Library of Congress Cataloging-in-Publication Data

Sease, Douglas.
   Winning with the market : beat the traders and brokers
      in good times and bad / Douglas R. Sease.
         p.   cm. — (A Wall Street journal book)
      1. Investments.   2. Portfolio management.
         3. Finance, Personal.   I. Title.   II. Series.
HG4521.S3578375 2001
332.6—dc21   00-052812
ISBN 0-7432-0416-6
      0-7432-0420-4 (Pbk)

FOR JANE

WINNING
WITH
THE MARKET

CONTENTS

How This Book Will Make You
a Better Investor

HERE'S THE DEFINING QUESTION to determine if you're an investor: Do you want the stock market to go up or down?

If you answered up, you're one of two things: retired and living on the proceeds of your investments, or a short-term trader looking to unload a position. If you're an investor—the person for whom this book is intended—you want the market to drop big and stay down for as long as you can invest new money. You know that's the only way to find lots of bargains and make lots of money over the long haul. Only when you're ready to be withdrawing money to support yourself in retirement do you want the market to rally.

But I'll be the first to admit that actually wishing for a big market drop is psychologically tough. I think back to the fall of 1998, when, after a period of astounding gains, the financial markets weren't doing so well. Russia had effectively defaulted on its government debt and thrown enough gasoline on the smoldering ruins of emerging markets to start a worldwide financial firestorm. The Dow Jones Industrial Average dropped nearly 20 percent from its peak, an event that had not occurred in several years. Small stocks were in a virtual depression, the market for initial public offerings was barren, and even the vast bond market had stalled, with the exception, of course, of the supersafe market for U.S. Treasury debt. The fallout from this market malaise spread rapidly. Big banks took heavy losses, hedge funds that had made huge and risky market bets were foundering, and the Federal Reserve was sufficiently frightened of the economic consequences that might follow that it quickly cut short-term interest rates to head off a recession. Fear was rampant.

What a great time that was to be buying stocks!

Yet what did I hear? Groans and moans from people who had seen their 401(k) plan balances drop 15 percent or so (and these were people who wouldn't be retiring for twenty or more years). Older investors who had been thinking about taking retirement started talking about staying around a few more years "until things get better." The only people who seemed to be enjoying life during that upsetting period were those who had most of their money invested in bonds and other safe investments. They took full advantage of the rare opportunity to gloat about how smart they were to avoid risky stocks.

There will always be an element of emotion involved in investing. After all, the nature of investing is to take risks seeking reward. As long as the rewards seem to far outweigh the risks, life is a bed of roses and account balances can rise to the sky. The only intelligent thing to do is put everything in stocks and bask in the riches that result. But when the risks seize the upper hand, as they inevitably will from time to time, panic sets in. Prices of everything are falling and can only fall further. There is no end in sight to the bad news. The same stocks that had you anticipating early retirement now seem like lead weights that must be cut loose if you're to survive financially. The all-too-frequent result of such emotional turmoil is this simple but disastrous formula: Buy high, sell low.

One key, then, to a successful investment program is to minimize the emotional component of investing. The better able you are to set aside emotions and act logically, the better your investment portfolio is going to perform over the years to come. This book is aimed at helping you temper the emotional roller coaster of investing.

Another key to a successful investment program is knowledge. But not the kind of knowledge you're thinking about. You probably want to be able to analyze a balance sheet and income statement of a company, figure out if some stock's price-earnings ratio is in line with those of other companies in the same industry, and project where interest rates are going. All that stuff is great if you're working on Wall Street and need to impress your clients. But that isn't the kind of knowledge I'm talking about. I'm much more interested that you know what can't be known. And that's easy: you can't know where stocks or interest rates are going. No matter how deeply you delve into business texts, no matter how many finance courses you take, and no matter how much some Wall Street brokerage firm is willing to pay you, the simple fact is that neither you nor anyone else knows what is going to happen to any single stock, to the overall stock market, or to interest rates. And if anyone tells you he can do these things, he's either lying or deluding himself. That's why I'm going to emphasize throughout this book that you do everything you can to avoid contact with the investment industry. I want you to enter a brokerless world where you make your own decisions free from the pressures and solicitations of people who will make money on your investments regardless of whether or not you do.

I'm not offering to make you a great investor. My very firm view is that it is exceedingly difficult to be a great investor. Peter Lynches and Warren Buffetts are few and far between. I don't know what makes them tick, and apparently nobody else does, either. People who try to emulate them come up short for some reason. And don't think that both Peter and Warren haven't made some bad calls. But it is my equally firm view that it isn't difficult at all to be a very good investor. There is no reason you cannot earn a healthy return on your investments, one that is consistent with your appetite for risk, if you simply understand that there are limits to what you can expect. And, perhaps as important, you won't waste hours of your time and thousands of your dollars in a futile effort to beat the market.

Presumably most of your investments will be made in U.S. financial markets. The U.S. stock market is the most efficient in the world. It is huge, highly liquid, well regulated, and thoroughly studied. What that means in practical terms is that it is well-nigh impossible for the average individual investor to know something about the value of a particular stock that somebody else hasn't already discovered and acted upon. The price you're quoted by a broker for a stock already reflects all that knowledge. Stocks that seem bargains usually deserve the price at which they're trading. Equally true, stocks that seem ludicrously overpriced also probably deserve the price at which they're trading.

I certainly don't mean to discourage you from investing. There are times when overall stock prices, responding to the overwhelming emotions that can grip millions of investors simultaneously, do fall to levels that are attractive. Certainly the crash of 1987 is one example. Those who steeled themselves to buy heavily in the aftermath of that plunge can look back on the crash as a seminal event in their portfolio's growth. And individual stocks can also be subject to emotional tumult, affording quick-witted investors a chance to buy at a reasonable price (or, better yet, to sell at an unreasonable price). But those occasions occur infrequently, and to wait until they occur is not a sound investment strategy.

I'd rather you go into investing with your eyes wide open, recognizing that it is unlikely that your stock and bond picks will outperform the overall market by any wide margin for any significant length of time. They certainly won't if you don't take careful account of the costs of investing — brokerage fees, research publications, and software, for example — or the tax consequences (Uncle Sam will gladly take up to 40 percent of any profits you make if you let him). More important, I want you to be able to minimize the amount of time you spend investing. You can't put a dollar figure on the hours wasted chasing hot stocks or the consequences of the stress on you and your family as markets and brokers whipsaw you around, only to leave you with subpar results. When you have finished this book, I hope you'll set your sights realistically and make every effort to become a good investor, not a great investor.

My wife, Jane, and I spend a lot of our free time on our sailboat *Galaxie*, ranging from the sandy shoals of the Bahamas to the rockbound coast of Maine. As a consequence we understand and appreciate the role of careful design and construction in building a seaworthy boat. Boats that endure the stresses of the ocean for years aren't thrown together willy-nilly. Rather, they reflect much forethought and an understanding of how they will be used, where they will go, and how much they will cost. One can't have all the latest electronic gadgets, the water toys, and the spaciousness of a floating palace without paying a high price. But one can have a fine boat that provides comfort, safety, and the ability to go anywhere in the world at a reasonable cost. My intention is to help you build a fine investment portfolio that will stand you in good stead for the rest of your life, no matter your age now. It will take time to build. Indeed, you'll be working on it for the rest of your life. But that isn't any less true of boats. Own one long enough and the engine needs to be replaced, the sails mended, ropes replaced, and the hull painted.

Like a boat, an investment portfolio can be as simple or as complex as you want. I have helped deliver big sailboats and even bigger powerboats up and down the East Coast. Some of the big motor yachts have been true marvels of engineering, design, power, and decor. The people who designed and built those boats were obviously very talented craftsmen. But the owners paid a huge price, not only to have the boats built, but to maintain and use them. Most of us have a hard enough time keeping up with simple suburban tract houses or two-bedroom co-ops and condos. We don't need such hugely complex and expensive objects, and that's true of our investments, too. A simple, low-cost portfolio can provide everything most of us need. There may be times and circumstances when you'll want to add some frills to your portfolio, and that's fine. Just know that they will invariably come at a cost and with a risk.

My ultimate aim is to free you from the tyranny of the financial services industry and the wasted time spent chasing outsize returns that only luck can produce. Part I is all about understanding and using the various vehicles—stocks, bonds, money managers, and mutual funds—to develop the most powerful and efficient portfolio you can while avoiding the psychological and emotional traps that Wall Street uses to get its hands in your pocketbook. Yet I begin in chapter 1 by urging you not to worry so much about controlling your investments as controlling your finances. I've been writing about investments and personal finance issues for years, and I hear frequently from people who, despite excellent incomes, are having immense difficulties with their finances. The problem is they're overreaching, trying to hit too many financial targets with too few dollars. You can't have an income of $100,000, spend $102,000, and have much left over for a disciplined and fruitful investment program. One common but dangerous solution that many people use is to try for outsize returns to make up for the lack of a steady flow of new money into their investment portfolios. I think that a successful long-term investment program is the result of, not a substitute for, a long-term approach to saving. Attempting to meet any financial goals through excessive returns on investments is a virtual guarantee of disappointment. Meeting those same goals through a disciplined savings program that funnels a steady stream of new money into an investment portfolio is a virtual guarantee of success, provided, of course, that the goals are reasonable in the first place. I'll show you in chapter 1 the rather dramatic effects that even small changes in spending, savings, and investment patterns can have on long-term investment results.

Chapter 2 discusses various aspects of stocks, which I think should be at the core of every investor's portfolio. Historically stocks have produced the best returns of any asset class, and the inherent nature of stocks—ownership of a company—certainly makes them the most interesting of assets. Not surprisingly, stocks are the arena in which financial professionals compete most fervently to capture your attention. Money managers and brokers bombard us constantly with their pitches, claiming to know which stocks to buy and sell, and they always have reasons that sound completely plausible. Many of us set out to emulate them, buying what they bought and selling what they sold. Yet when one examines the performance of most money managers, they aren't even capable of matching the performance of simple stock market indexes. Even the best, who consistently outperform the indexes (there aren't many), make big mistakes, buying stocks that drop in value or ignoring those that soon rise. As I noted earlier, the stock market is an incredibly efficient place. It is virtually impossible in most circumstances to know something about any given stock that will give you a leg up on all the professionals who are paid millions of dollars each year to figure out which stocks to buy or sell. I'll discuss in nonacademic terms the efficient market hypothesis and how that should govern your approach to stocks and the stock market.

Stocks are the vehicle I think you should use to *accumulate* wealth. Bonds are the vehicle I think you should use to *preserve* wealth. While stocks should be the core of any long-term investor's portfolio, bonds are a second essential ingredient. The very word *bond* sounds safe and secure. And bonds should be used as a safety net in your portfolio, to offset the occasional shocks that occur when stocks get clobbered, either justly or unjustly. In your overall investment portfolio bonds play the role of the control rods in a nuclear reactor, tempering the speed of the reactions to keep everyone safe but not slowing them so much that no energy is produced. But not all bonds are created equal. You can buy U.S. Trea-

sury bonds, which are considered by most experts to be the safest
investment in the world. Or you can be greedy and reach for
higher yields, only to wind up saddled with a portfolio of aptly
named "junk bonds." And while the bond market seems to many
investors to be much more staid than the hyperkinetic stock market, don't be fooled: there's plenty of volatility in bond prices and
plenty of unscrupulous dealers are trying to wrest money out of
your wallet in the guise of selling safety. Indeed, the bond market
remains the most opaque financial market in the United States,
where prices are a secret held closely by the insiders. In chapter 3
I'll discuss a variety of approaches to keeping your wealth safe and
point out what's wrong with each. I'll give you my own recommendation—inflation-indexed Treasury bonds—while freely acknowledging that it's far from perfect. I just think T-bonds are
better than anything else at protecting what you've accumulated.

As you accumulate financial assets a lot of people are going to
want to help you manage your money. Indeed, I'm one of them.
As it turns out, I'm willing to charge you a lot less than most of the
others, and I think my advice is better than theirs. But that will be
for you to decide. Chapter 4, "Money Managers and Mutual
Funds," gives you my take on the financial services world. My obvious bias is toward mutual funds. There are good reasons that so
many people love mutual funds. Simplicity. Diversity. Low costs.
What stocks were to an earlier generation, mutual funds are to
today's investors. The relative merits of various Internet funds can
occupy entire dinner conversations. People are always wanting to
know—and any number of pundits are always willing to say—
what mutual funds they should own. Today. As opposed to yester-
day. Mutual funds have become something to be bought for quick
gains and discarded when the gains end in favor of some other
fund that's on the rise. In their quest to win more of the vast sums
flowing into the mutual fund industry, the funds themselves en-
courage this short-term view. Some funds are even priced hourly
for those in the trading crowd who dart into and out of them, and
there has recently been a proliferation of exchange-traded funds,
which you can buy and sell instantly just like stocks. But investors
using mutual funds in that way run head-on into the same problem that confronts them in the stock market: Which funds are
going to provide the best returns?

The answer: Nobody knows. Which is why I'm a hearty advocate of index mutual funds. You'll never beat the market with an index fund for the simple reason that the index fund *is* the market. But you'll never do worse than the market, either (well, maybe a tiny bit worse since index funds have administrative costs that the indexes don't). And by choosing index funds, you're instantly free of the time spent trying to figure out which funds will be hot and free from the costs of paying the high salaries of fund managers who can't routinely beat the indexes.

I'll admit right now that taking control of your investments isn't going to be very exciting if you do it my way, free of brokers and hassles. And you're constantly going to be reading or hearing about all kinds of tempting ways to make big bucks fast. But in every case I know of, these investing fads have come and gone, leaving only their promoters significantly better off. The current rage is day trading, which involves jumping quickly into and out of a stock to capture gains. The people who do well—and the firms that rent them space and equipment and handle their trades— love to brag about how much money they're making. I think their memories are probably very selective, conveniently recalling the victories, easily forgetting the defeats. And every time I hear or read about these people, they're telling us the price at which they bought the stock and then sold it. What they're aren't telling us is the size of their tax bill, the trading commissions, and the interest rate on the loans that many take out to fund their foray into trading. Add all those costs, and the returns aren't nearly as good as they sounded at first. And, of course, the players who do poorly mostly just slink quietly away, although at least one has gone berserk and killed colleagues.

Part II of the book introduces you to what is probably the single most important concept you need to understand: asset allocation. That's just a fancy term to describe the process of balancing your investment portfolio among cash, stocks, and bonds to suit your own lifestyle, your financial goals, and your tolerance for risk. It's far more important to get this part right than to figure out which mutual funds or stocks to buy. And asset allocation is a dynamic process. If you follow my advice about saving money as a source of fuel for your investment program, you'll need to think from time to time about where that new money is being invested. Maybe your goals change, maybe your income changes. In either case you'll want to adjust your asset allocation. Even if you do nothing after making an initial investment, the balance in your portfolio will shift over time as one asset outperforms another. That, too, will trigger the need to make some adjustments. I also show you how to view your financial life in its entirety rather than as a collection of stocks, bonds, and mutual funds. An understanding of your total financial picture can make a big difference in how you allocate money among various investment vehicles.

I approach the question of asset allocation through the creation of hypothetical portfolios that demonstrate the principles of conscientious saving and investing. I could reduce all of this part of the book to just three actions: Get invested. Stay invested. Add to your investments. While anyone following that advice would do very well, the truth is that individual circumstances vary enormously and affect how each of us would go about accomplishing those three goals. Since individual circumstances would produce nearly infinite variations in how to build an investment portfolio, I've chosen to present options based mostly on an investor's age. Although not infallible, age usually correlates fairly well with income level, investment time horizon, and certain financially significant events, such as home purchases, college education, and the ultimate goal, retirement. Thus I have devoted separate chapters to new investors getting started at different times in their lives. The portfolios are developed roughly around decade-long intervals. There are suggested approaches for people in their twenties, thirties, forties, and fifties and those who are already or almost retired. I know that you'll want to turn immediately to the chapter that covers your age bracket, and that's fine. Read it first. But then go back and peruse chapters aimed at investors both younger and older than yourself. In each case you'll probably find some advice that might be useful to you at your age—or that you can tuck away to make use of five or ten years from now.

At the end of the book you'll find "An Investor's Tool Kit." It contains helpful information about what I believe are the best index funds to use to achieve your financial goals. It also contains a directory of Federal Reserve banks and branches that will help you set up a Treasury Direct account to buy Treasury bonds at government auctions. More important, there are tools in the tool kit that will allow you to do some "what if" planning. They'll help you calculate how much money you might amass over the years and how much you can afford to spend once you're in retirement.

The Tool Kit also provides the URL—www.winning.wsj.com —that will take those of you familiar with the Internet to some more interactive planning tools to further test some financial scenarios.

There are two lessons that I hope will become very clear in the simple portfolios I have constructed in part II. The first is that the earlier you begin investing, the easier and the more lucrative it will be. Yet young people don't understand the value of making even small investments when they're in their twenties, and people nearing retirement who haven't paid much attention to their finances realize too late just how difficult it will be to accomplish their goals. The second lesson is that stocks are the best way to accomplish long-term financial goals. If you compare my approach to investing with that offered by many financial advisers, you'll find I'm in favor of holding larger portions of your wealth in stocks. I believe stocks will get you where you're going faster and give you a bigger cushion when you get there.

Are there risks in this approach? Absolutely! Stocks are volatile and unpredictable. While I use past performance as a guide to what you might expect, there isn't any guarantee whatsoever that stocks will continue to perform as they have in the past. Certainly you can't expect stocks to deliver the 20 percent or more in annual returns they did in the late 1990s. But my point is that there are risks in *any* approach to investing. You could, for instance, put all your money in government-insured bank accounts. But you would be running an enormous risk that inflation would destroy that money's value over time, leaving you sadly wanting when it comes time to retire. Given that we all have to make a bet, I'm willing to bet that stocks will continue to be the single best place to invest for periods of ten years or more. If you're uncomfortable with the proportions of stocks that I recommend, that's fine. You can always temper your portfolio by shifting a larger proportion of it to bonds. But you must accept that you'll likely have lower long-term returns that may affect your ability to reach your long-term goals.

There will be numerous temptations along the way to investment success. Many of them will be laid before you by the financial services industry, always eager to find a way to get its hand in your pocketbook. But some of them will simply arise out of your innate curiosity. You might be tempted, for instance, to try to analyze the nation's economy, the overall stock market, or even individual stocks. At the very least you'll probably be reading a newspaper (I hope it's *The Wall Street Journal*) and will come across economic and corporate news and analysis. If you wanted to—or if you were being paid to—you could spend all day every day parsing the thousands of economic and market statistics that pour from government and the financial services industry and putting your own spin on news events. But then you'd be right back where you didn't want to be, devoting precious time to endeavors that almost certainly aren't worth the effort. I'll make it easy by putting things in perspective for you. The answer to the question "How bad can it get?" is pretty scary until you know the answer to a second question: "How likely is it to get that bad?" Not very.

When you're finished with this book, put it on your bookshelf. Avoid the temptation to give it to your children, your brother, or a good friend. Or to throw it away. Come back to it from time to time, especially in times of market turmoil, when you may be doubting your own wisdom in setting up your portfolio the way you have. The United States has enjoyed an unprecedented span of prosperity that has drawn millions of people into the stock and bond markets, and I'm delighted about that. Yet each day that passes means we're all one day closer to the next big market disruption, and a true bear market will doubtless convince many investors that they've made a huge mistake by investing in stocks. But if you have used this book correctly to understand the basics of the investment process and to tailor your portfolio to your own needs, you will have the confidence to weather that storm. You may want to do some fine-tuning in times of trouble, but remember that a well-built house can stand up to the tests of time with the proper maintenance and care. So will your portfolio.

PART ONE

LESSONS FOR LONG-TERM INVESTORS

1

SUPERCHARGING YOUR PORTFOLIO WITH SAVINGS

THERE ARE JUST TWO THINGS you can do with money: spend it or save it. We all know very well how to spend it. None of us needs any books or courses on that topic. But in years of studying and writing about personal finance, I can attest that many of us—and I was certainly guilty for an uncomfortably large part of my adult life—don't know much about saving money. This is a book about investing, and there's going to be plenty in it about how to get the best returns on the money you invest. But the return you get is just one part of the equation that leads to amassing more wealth than you probably dreamed possible. The other part of that equation is the ability to save more money to invest. Savings is the fuel that supercharges an investment portfolio and can make the difference between reaching and exceeding financial goals and falling woefully short. Put another way, given two people with the same income and the same investment portfolio, the one who makes a diligent effort to save money could, under the right circumstances, retire years earlier than the one who pays close attention to the investment side of the equation but ignores the savings side. Of course, not everyone wants to retire early. But the point is that the person who saves and invests will have much more control of his or her life than the one who simply invests without any thought of how to feed more fuel to his or her portfolio. The ability to save is nothing less than freedom.

Saving isn't easy. It requires discipline, knowledge, and fore-thought. An effective saver is able to forgo the instant, but often short-lived, gratification of spending money now. Becoming an effective saver requires knowledge about the flow of money into and out of your life, something amazingly few people know much about. Finally, effective savings requires the ability to plan ahead to avoid unpleasant—and costly—surprises in your financial life. Done properly, saving becomes a habit that is hard to kick. The instant gratification of making an impulse purchase is supplanted by the much more deeply satisfying comfort of being financially secure. The knowledge of how money is flowing through your life provides a sense of control unknown to people living from one paycheck to the next. And the ability to plan for most of life's contingencies—college educations, home purchases, travel, and, ultimately, retirement—makes it possible to weather the genuinely unexpected upsets that afflict all our lives—illness, job loss, divorce—if not with aplomb, then with considerably less anxiety.

TACTICAL SAVING

I've found it useful to think about saving money in much the way military officers think about conducting warfare. There are *tactics*—developing and executing a short-term plan, such as capturing an important bridge—that are part of a much larger plan, or *strategy*, such as winning the war. Tactical savings is all about creating the conditions in which you keep more of the money that comes to you as salary. It's a battle that literally is fought every day. It requires constant vigilance and attention to detail. It's a battle you don't win every day. Like a good commander, you need to know when to push ahead, but you also need to know when to retreat in the face of overwhelming odds. Strategic savings is about winning the financial war. The objective: long-term financial security. Achieving that objective takes time. The battle is measured in years and decades. And again, you don't win all the time. There will be setbacks that can be unnerving. But those setbacks will be much less painful than they would be were you not fighting the war and simply overrun by financial circumstances.

Without tactics you can't execute a strategy. So we'll start our savings campaign on the front lines, where paychecks come head-to-head with the temptations of spending. For most of us, income is a more or less fixed thing. We're paid so much per week or per month, and there simply isn't any more that we can obtain, short of getting a second job. Against that fixed supply of money flowing into our lives on a regular basis we have a highly variable outflow, only some of which can be controlled easily. We all know the basic expenses: food, shelter, and clothing. Since those are the necessities of life, you might be tempted to think of them as fixed costs. And to the extent that you have to have all three to survive, they are fixed. But there's also a huge variable content to each of those expenditures. To view the extremes, either you can heat up a can of beans (actually, cold beans aren't that bad) or you can obtain your nourishment at an upscale restaurant. You can live in a studio apartment or you can have an oceanfront mansion. And you can dress in T-shirts and shorts or have several closets full of suits and shoes and chests full of jewelry. But I'm not an extremist, and you probably aren't, either. For most of us there is a middle ground for obtaining food, shelter, and clothing. Where in that middle ground you choose to make your stand will determine to some extent how much of that fixed sum of money coming to you periodically you can divert to savings and, from there, to investing.

After the basic necessities are taken care of, our options for spending money become much more variable and, to some extent, more unpredictable. Take, for example, how we entertain ourselves. A night of television or a night at a Broadway show? A weekend on the local ski slopes or a trip out west to ski the Rockies? A formal dinner party for a dozen or a couple of friends over for pizza and beer? Then there are the unpredictable events: the roof develops a leak or your car engine overheats and seizes up. Those kinds of setbacks can take a big chunk out of your income, at least temporarily.

The first objective of tactical savings is to rein in as many of those variable expenses as possible to ensure that, on average, we take in more over a given period of time than we spend. As surprising as it may seem, very few people know if they're achieving that objective. The spectacular rise in personal bankruptcy filings over the past decade is proof that hundreds of thousands of people were spending money much faster than they were bringing it in. And the even more spectacular rise in credit card debt over that same period suggests that millions more have been spending at least a little more than they've been taking in every year. Indeed, if you regularly carry over a monthly balance on a credit card, you should consider yourself in need of some increased spending discipline.

Once that first objective is attained, the second objective of tactical savings becomes increasing the amount we are able to save. Finding an additional $25 or $50 a week that can be saved doesn't sound like a very big accomplishment. But as we'll see later, when it is invested and compounded over a long period of time, achieving that little victory can make a huge difference in the outcome of the war to win financial freedom.

Modern savers, like modern military commanders, have an awesome array of tools available to them these days to accomplish their objectives, principally computer software. Compared to what we had before the advent of the personal computer, it's a fabulous weapon that can be very effective in helping us plan our financial future. But just as in warfare, technology doesn't solve all problems. Somebody still has to be in the trenches. And, at least in the first several months of formulating a tactical savings plan, that person is *you!* I've found that the problem with financial software is that it doesn't capture sufficient detail for you to become intimately familiar with your own spending habits. Sure, it tracks the checks you write, the deposits you make, and the other details of your finances that it can obtain from various sources. What it doesn't do is track specific purchases. While a software program records a check of $670 to Visa or MasterCard, it doesn't record the details of the various transactions that added up to that $670 bill. And when you're getting serious about savings, the devil is very definitely in the details.

I'm a perfect example of how that lack of detail can be fatal, or nearly so. Back in the bad old days before I discovered the joys of the public library, my monthly book purchase bills totaled a few hundred dollars. Add to that the pleasures of charging a few restaurant meals, and I easily had monthly charge card balances running $1,000 or more. Yet I didn't really know where I had spent all that money. And I certainly didn't balance those charge bills and various other expenses against my weekly take-home pay. Thus it came as a complete surprise to me that I was living far beyond my means. Fortunately that revelation didn't come as the result of having to declare personal bankruptcy or from losing my house through foreclosure. Rather, it came one day when it dawned on me that $20,000 I had banked two years earlier from the profitable sale of a house had simply *disappeared.* I couldn't begin to explain where it had gone. That inability to explain, even just to myself, how I had lost $20,000 while earning a perfectly good salary was frightening. It was enough of a jolt to spur me to formulate a plan to figure out where every penny that I was spending was going and to bring the balance of inflow and outflow at least back to equilibrium. That's when I discovered the three-by-five index card, a weapon for the saver that is the equivalent of the infantryman's rifle.

In my near religious fervor to find out what was happening to my money, I began carrying an index card with me wherever I went. And much to my wife's dismay, I imposed my new discipline on her, too. Anytime we spent any money on anything—whether it was a quarter for a pack of gum, $200 for a new suit, or the $950 monthly house payment—the amount and the reason were set down on the card under the specific date. But it wasn't just spending that we recorded. We also noted each time we received our paychecks how much take-home pay we had. I noted, too, when the bank posted interest income to our checking account. I even had the good fortune to find a $5 bill lying in the street, a sum that I dutifully entered on the income side of that day's index card ledger.

The results were astounding. Based on the first few weeks of data, I could easily see that restaurant meals were killing us and book purchases were causing considerable financial pain. As soon as I realized how much we were spending on those two items, we applied the brakes. Within two months I began to feel that our finances weren't hopelessly out of balance. And other aspects of our financial picture became clearer, too. Impulse purchases of things like magazines, clothes, sporting goods, and compact discs took a toll on our bank account, although not as large or regularly as eating out or buying books. There were also the occasional but necessary big hits, such as semiannual car insurance bills. Those sorts of things simply aren't captured by a review of the checks you've written over the last month, which is a common prescription for getting at least a basic grasp of your cash flow.

Recording each and every expenditure sounds like an enormous amount of work. But it really isn't. It takes only a moment to jot down each expense and less than half an hour each month to tally the results of income and spending to determine how far ahead or behind you are. But the act of recording each expenditure has benefits that far outweigh the minor inconvenience. Not only do you gain immense knowledge about your spending habits and financial picture, but the simple thought of knowing you must record a purchase gives you just a second to think twice about making the purchase. We found early on that things we would have bought on a whim became much less important to us if we gave the proposed transaction that momentary second thought. And it doesn't take long to fall into the habit of making that quick judgment each time. Should you follow this method, you'll probably be surprised at how many times you opt to not buy something and how seldom you regret not buying it (if you really do regret it, you can almost always go back and buy it later).

I know, using an index card in this digital age sounds hopelessly primitive. And if you find that using a PalmPilot or some other electronic device to record your income and outgo works better for you, that's fine (each time I think about buying one, my second-thought reflex kicks in and I decide, "Not yet"). Just be sure that using your personal digital assistant is easy enough that you actually record each purchase on the spot, not three or four hours later. The mind—at least my mind—has an impressive ability to forget minor transactions within minutes of their completion. Trying to recall each evening what I spent during the course of the day simply didn't work.

While tactical savings takes place day to day, you'll nevertheless need to make a long-term commitment to doing it because it is at the heart of strategic savings, which is a vital component of any long-term investment program. You needn't use index cards for the rest of your life. Once the habit of thinking twice about any given purchase becomes ingrained, you will have attained the major objective of tactical savings. But expenses and income will ebb and flow over the course of time, especially expenses. Your expense profile will change remarkably at certain turning points in your life, particularly if you have children. When you undergo some major change that affects your financial life, break out the index cards for a few more months. Knowing how such changes are affecting your finances will enable you to weather them with the least disruption. And that is the goal of strategic savings. The discipline developed in tactical savings gives you the advantage you need to obtain the major objective of strategic savings, which is to keep new money flowing into your long-term investment portfolio. The amount that you contribute to new investments may rise and fall over time, but the important thing is to keep *something* flowing into the portfolio.

STRATEGIC SAVINGS: OPPORTUNITY COSTS AND MENTAL MONEY

Tactical savings involves lots of little details but doesn't require much thinking. Strategic savings is a much broader concept. It doesn't deal much in detail. Rather, it's all about how you *think* about saving and where it fits into your financial life. It requires you to decide how you're going to save and how you're going to spend. At its heart it is all about a concept called "opportunity costs," which is a fancy term for deciding which of the two things you can do with money you're going to do: spend it or save it.

We all think we're reasonably familiar with what things cost. Usually there's a price tag or we get a bill that tells us the cost. If you practice my version of tactical savings, what something costs is the amount you write down each time you spend money on something. But the truth is, the cost of most things that we buy is considerably higher than what the price tag says it costs. That's because each time you elect to spend a dollar, you're simultaneously electing not to invest that dollar. And a dollar invested is almost always worth more than a dollar spent. The only exception is if the thing you spent the dollar for increases in value. The increase can be explicit: an antique desk or a fine painting may appreciate in value over the years. Or it can be implicit: a dollar spent for education will likely provide excellent, though un-known, returns over the years. But most things on which we spend money—clothing, entertainment, automobiles—either depreci-ate in value or provide only a brief sense of contentment. If a dol-lar is saved and subsequently invested in a long-term portfolio, however, it will almost certainly become more valuable over time. How much more valuable will depend on the nature of the invest-ment. The concept of opportunity costs measures the cost of spending as the sum total of the actual price paid for something plus the forgone gains that would have accrued had that dollar been invested rather than spent.

Let's take a look at an example of how opportunity cost analy-sis works on a big-ticket item. Let's say you've had your Toyota Camry for five years now and you're starting to think about buy-ing a new one. To make our example simple, we'll assume you'll keep the old Camry, perhaps giving it to your daughter to use at college. A visit to your local car dealer shows you can buy a new one for about $25,000. Because you're a savvy saver, you in-tend to pay cash rather than rack up all those financing charges by borrowing to buy the new car, so the cost really appears to be $25,000, not $25,000 plus four or five years of finance charges. But what happens if you decide you can get another five years of use out of your current Camry (your daughter probably needs to study more and drive less, anyway)? Now you have $25,000 to invest that would have gone for the car. We'll assume that you invest in stocks that provide an average annual return of 10 per-cent, a little less than the historical average return for a diversified portfolio of stocks. Five years from now, when you're thinking about a new car again, you'll have $40,263: the $25,000 you didn't spend on the car five years earlier and another $15,263 you earned on that $25,000. The opportunity cost of buying that new Camry is more than $40,000, not the $25,000 you saw on the window sticker.

Of course, in the real world it isn't that simple. Stocks may go into a slump and return something less than 10 percent annually (or they may soar and return quite a bit more). If you invest in something that produces a lower annual return than stocks, the opportunity cost of buying the new car won't be as high. And over the next five years the price of a new Camry will almost certainly rise, so that you'll wind up paying more for a new car than you would if you bought it today. If you're doing a really thorough analysis, you'll want to assign some amount to the maintenance and repair of the old car if you decide to keep it, and if you buy the new one, you'll want to assign some value to it as a trade-in five years from now. But the point remains: The new car almost certainly will cost substantially more than the sticker price if you could otherwise have invested that money. It isn't an accident that a study of the personalities and habits of millionaires found a disproportionate number driving old cars. That's partly how they became millionaires!

Big-ticket items like cars make it easy to see the difference between spending and investing a certain sum of money. But the principle works on small-ticket stuff, too. Take the seemingly trivial purchase of a $15 compact disc. If that $15 were invested at an average annual return of 10 percent, it would be worth $25 five years from now.

That brings us to another point about opportunity costs: They can be measured over any period of time. In the case of the cars we just examined, we're assuming you'll need a new car at some point, and it isn't unreasonable to think you can get ten years of life out of a high-quality car that isn't abused. That's why we figured the opportunity cost over five years (the old car is already five years old, and your choice is to buy a new one or keep the old one another five years). But let's look at a different situation, again involving cars. This time you're going to consider buying a $17,000 Toyota Corolla as an alternative to the $25,000 Camry. Again assuming a 10 percent return if you invested the money, the Corolla has an opportunity cost of $27,379 (the $17,000 price tag plus $10,379 in forgone investment returns) over five years. So what looks like a cost difference of $8,000 between the sticker prices of the two cars is really a difference of $12,884 when the five-year opportunity costs are compared.

But don't stop there. Because you elected to buy a cheaper car (and presumably will eventually replace it with yet another relatively "cheap" car), the $8,000 you saved by choosing the Corolla instead of the Camry needn't ever be spent; rather, it's what we'll call "permanent savings." So you can feel free to invest that amount in stocks returning an average of 10 percent for as long as you wish. Invest it for twenty years and you'll have $53,820. Invest it for thirty years and you'll have an amazing $139,595. Now how much would that Camry really cost you? Even the $15 compact disc has an astounding opportunity cost—$101 at twenty years and $262 at thirty years—if you choose to invest the $15 rather than spend it. The process works in the short term, too. Delaying the purchase of the $25,000 car one year gives you $2,500 in investment returns at 10 percent.

Don't get the wrong idea. I'm not trying to condemn anyone to living in a cave wearing animal skins and eating only what food can be trapped or grown outside the cave. As I said before, I'm not an extremist, and neither are you. Opportunity cost analysis is merely a tool to be used in thinking about spending and saving. Once you have a more realistic picture of what things cost, you will be able to think more carefully about how important any given expenditure is in the overall scheme of things and possibly consider alternatives, such as a less expensive new car or a late-model used car.

Here's a simple question: What's a dollar worth? The answer could be phrased different ways—100 pennies, 20 nickels, 10 dimes, or maybe 4 quarters—but it amounts to the same thing: A dollar is worth one dollar. Surely you agree with that statement. But if you do, why do you value one dollar more highly than another dollar? And you almost surely do. We all do. It's a human tendency that scholarly folks called behavioral economists have long known about, although they don't completely understand why it happens. Here's an example: Suppose you want to buy a new stereo system and you find one you like priced at $500 at a store one mile from your house. But before you buy it, you see a newspaper ad showcasing the exact same system at a store in the next town, twenty-five miles away, for $400. Would you drive thirty minutes to save that $100? If you're like me, you certainly would.

Now instead of shopping for a new stereo system, let's go shopping for a new car, perhaps that Camry we were just using as an example. Your nearby dealer will sell it for $25,000. But a dealer in the neighboring town twenty-five miles away advertises that he will sell the exact same car for $24,900. Will you drive thirty minutes to save $100? If you're like me, probably not. But why not? You're saving exactly $100 in exchange for a thirty-minute drive in both cases. Why is one $100 saving less valuable—that is, not worth a thirty-minute drive—when the other

$100 saving is worth the drive? "Human nature" is about the only answer we can come up with.

Behavioral economists refer to this kind of thinking as creating "mental accounts." They point out that the value we place on any given dollar depends on the source of the money and where it fits into our mental picture of our finances. Money that comes to us as salary is somehow more valuable than money that comes to us in the form of a tax refund or a gift. Many of us actually create separate accounts: there's the savings account aimed at making a down payment on a house, there's a "clothes budget," and, of course, there are our retirement accounts. Fortunately, most of us value a dollar in our retirement accounts or in our "house budget" more highly than we value a dollar in our clothes budget or a dollar riding around in our purse or wallet, even though the value in the real world is exactly the same. Such mental gymnastics help us reach our financial goals, and if that's what it takes, fine.

But mental accounts can also be hazardous to our financial health. Credit cards are a good example. Studies have shown that people value a dollar in their wallet much more highly than they value a dollar spent on a credit card purchase. In other words, it's a lot easier for many of us to buy that $400 stereo with our Visas or MasterCards than with a wad of cash, even though the total expenditure is exactly the same. Somehow signing a charge slip for $400 doesn't equate in our minds with spending forty $10 bills. Worse still, some of us value the dollars in our savings account so highly that we will continue to let them sit there earning 3 percent while we assign such a low value to charge card dollars that we carry a credit card balance that is costing us 18 percent. Smart investors deplete the savings account to pay off the charge debt and come out 15 percent ahead in the process. Becoming a strategic saver is all about realizing when mental accounts can be helpful—budgeting for a new car or retirement years in advance—and when they can be harmful.

UNDERSTANDING DEBT:
THE GOOD AND THE BAD

One of the principal goals of strategic savings is to avoid debt. The opportunity costs alone of any given purchase are high enough without adding the extra burden of financing charges. Take the $25,000 Camry again. If instead of buying it for cash you put down $5,000 and finance the remaining $20,000 for five years at 10 percent, the interest charges alone total $5,496. That puts the total cost of the car at $30,496 before you even begin to calculate the opportunity cost. Admittedly, figuring the opportunity cost gets complicated if you assume you don't have the $25,000 in cash to invest and would instead invest an initial $5,000 (the amount you would have put down on the car) and another $424.94 each month (the equivalent of the monthly payment on your car loan). But rest assured it's considerably higher than if you paid cash for the car.

The strategic saver's knowledge of family income and out-flow over a period of time provides the important flexibility to plan ahead for such things as car purchases, college educations, and big vacation trips (remember, I'm no extremist; I like vacations and take my fair share). More important, however, the constant accumulation of money in the family's coffers provides a safety net for the unexpected expenses that invariably occur. Without that safety net many people wind up borrowing on their credit cards or otherwise going deeper into debt, a process that makes it increasingly difficult to regain their financial footing. In your case that won't be a problem since you're obviously intent on tak-ing control of your own investments. But the cushion of extra cash in a savings account does help you avoid the periodic or occasional selling of some of your investments to meet temporary cash crunches. If your investment portfolio consists mostly of stocks—and that's what I'll recommend as we get further into this text—you'll enjoy one of the huge advantages stocks offer: com-pounding of returns free of most taxes until you actually sell the stocks. Having to sell some of your stocks to meet temporary cash demands will often incur a tax liability that, in the long run, will hurt your investment performance. Better to plan ahead—and save ahead—to meet obligations than to be constantly tapping what should be your long-term investment portfolio.

While most debt is a true burden to your financial health, not all debt is bad debt. I made the point earlier that borrowing to get the best education possible will almost certainly carry great—although incalculable—returns over a lifetime. Mortgage debt, however, brings a much more concrete return and represents the best example of how a strategic saver needs to think about spending and saving. I know lots of people who make it their financial goal to pay off their mortgages, which sounds like a noble enough goal until you begin to think strategically about it. Mortgage debt is one of the few kinds of debt that the U.S. government encourages through the tax system. Because mortgage interest is a deductible item on federal and most state income tax returns, it can be the cheapest money you will ever be able to borrow. Just how cheap depends on your tax bracket, of course. For those in the highest federal tax brackets, the cost of borrowing money to buy a house or condominium is about 40 percent less than the stated interest rate of the loan. When these people take out an 8 percent mortgage, for example, they're really paying interest at the rate of just 4.8 percent or less. If they can expect to earn the average 10 percent or so that stocks return each year over the life of their thirty-year mortgage, they'll have a net return of 5.2 percent on the money they owe the mortgage lender. Let's figure the opportunity cost on that by looking at the purchase of a $240,000 house. You could, if you've been a good saver, pay cash. Or, if you've been a good saver, you could put down 20 percent, take an 8 percent mortgage for the remaining $200,000, and invest your own $200,000 in stocks. Thirty years later, when the house is paid off, you'll have $915,171 in your stock portfolio as well as a paid-for house. Again, the analysis gets trickier if you don't have the $220,000 in cash but have to make monthly contributions to your investment fund. The effect, however, is still to accumulate large sums of money with Uncle Sam's help. Of course, for those in lower tax brackets, the opportunity cost of financing a mortgage and investing the balance is less.

Now let's carry our strategic thinking a little further. If you've ever looked at mortgage amortization tables that depict what portion of each month's house payment goes to paying the mortgage interest and what portion goes to reducing the principal amount of the loan, you'll notice that in the first ten years or so a huge chunk goes to pay the interest on the loan. In the last ten years of a thirty-year loan a much larger proportion of each payment goes to reducing the principal. The net result is that the longer you keep the mortgage loan, the less of that government-subsidized money you have. And that's why I recommend that you begin to reconsider refinancing your home at the ten-year mark. Of course, many of us move from one city to another during the course of our careers, in effect being forced to refinance a mortgage each time. But if you find yourself settled in at one location for a decade or more, at least give some consideration to letting Uncle Sam subsidize your investment program by refinancing that house.

While some mortgage debt is fine, too much can be bad. Don't be so eager to take on tax-subsidized mortgage debt that you have no additional cash flow to devote to saving and investing. That can happen if a 20 percent down payment eats up your available cash and the monthly payments on the mortgage eat up everything left after the basic necessities. That's carrying the example too far. And while real estate is a legitimate asset class for investors, don't convince yourself to buy more house than you can afford with the rationale that you're "investing" that money. Investing in real estate as an asset class requires knowledge of projected returns from rents and sales and some degree of geographical diversification, if not across regions, then at least in different sections of a town or city. A single house simply doesn't meet the criteria for being an investment: it is highly illiquid (difficult and expensive to sell), returns cannot be projected adequately, and it is at the mercy of what happens to your neighborhood and the local real estate market. Buy a house to live in because you like the location, the design, or the neighborhood, but don't substitute the house for a real investment program.

MAKING YOUR SAVINGS WORK FOR YOU

Saving is not the same thing as investing. Investing is a long-term concept, measured in returns over years and aimed at achieving the maximum possible returns consistent with your risk tolerance. Saving, on the other hand, is a short-term concept, measured in months. Think of the money you're saving as sitting in a waiting room from which it eventually will be summoned either to be spent on some unusual expense or to be tucked away in a long-term investment portfolio. You want the money you save to be liquid (easily obtainable) and stable (you want always to know how much you've got and how much you're going to have at some given date in the future, absent extraordinary expenses). There are several places you can stash your savings while you're waiting to deploy it to its higher and better use. The most obvious place is in a bank checking account or savings account or the equivalent at a credit union or savings and loan institution. They're insured by the federal government for losses up to $100,000, and that's an appealing thought to many conservative savers. But the price you pay for that insurance—in the form of very low interest earnings—is awfully steep. Bank certificates of deposit (CDs), especially longer-term CDs, offer much better interest rates. My objection to them is that you're required to deposit the money for a specified period of time up to five years. There goes the liquidity you wanted unless you plan well ahead (I've got a solution that will let you earn those higher rates yet still retain a healthy measure of liquidity; more about that shortly).

That leaves us with what I believe is far and away the best "waiting room" in which to park your money: money market funds. The "money market" is a term to describe the short-term borrowing by the government and corporations to meet their continuing needs for cash. Because the loans are of very short terms—typically 30 to 270 days—it's too much trouble for the borrowers to go to the public as they do when they sell bonds or issue stock. Instead they arrange to borrow from big financial institutions. Mutual funds, with their ability to pool huge amounts of money from us little guys, play in that market, and we're the beneficiaries. A money market fund takes our money and lends it to the government or a company at a certain interest rate. When the note is paid off, the mutual fund keeps some of the interest that was earned on the loan and passes the rest of it on to us. Typically money market funds pay higher rates on our deposits than do banks, thrifts, or credit unions. However, the money you send to a money market fund isn't insured by the government even if the fund invests in U.S. Treasury securities (which have virtually no risk of default). That disturbs some investors, but the fact is that money market funds, even those that invest in corporate debt, typically are so well diversified that a default by one or even a few borrowers will have little or no impact on the overall health of the fund. And in cases in which funds have been heavily exposed to a default, the management of the fund has stepped in to bail out the shareholders. Although such bailouts aren't required, the fund management knows that it would be out of business if it allowed the default to take money out of the hands of the shareholders. If you can get past the lack of government insurance, you can invest in a range of money market funds, from government funds that feature the security of U.S. Treasury obligations (and the lower interest rates that are commensurate with the lack of risk) to corporate funds that strive for higher returns at the risk of a borrower or two defaulting.

How do you pick the right money market fund for you? I'm going to have a lot more to say about the costs of investing later in the book, but this is a good time to emphasize my central point: Costs—how much a mutual fund, a money manager, or a broker charges you for services—matter a lot more than most people think. The money market is a highly competitive arena in which the borrowers are shopping for the lowest interest rate they can get and the lenders—in our case whichever money market funds we are shopping among—are competing against one another to offer the highest yields to attract our money. Within any given category of money market fund, but especially among corporate money market funds, there are only two ways to improve the yield offered to savers: take more risk or cut administrative costs. Companies in serious financial trouble are obviously willing to—indeed, must— pay higher rates to borrow in the money market. A money market fund can markedly improve the interest rate it pays to shareholders by lending to companies with lower credit ratings. I've already said that the risk of sending money to most money market funds isn't something you have to worry much about, and that's especially true of funds offered by the big fund families like Vanguard, Fidelity, and T. Rowe Price, among others. But if you can get the same, or nearly the same, yield from a fund that takes less risk, why not choose that one? And how does that fund offer the same yield without taking the same risks? Simple: It has lower costs. Here's how it works. If one fund has costs of .50 percent and another has costs of .20 percent, the higher-cost fund must find borrowers that will pay .30 percent more than the lower-cost fund just to offer the same yield to investors. Now .30 percent doesn't sound like much, but it can mean millions of dollars of extra expense to companies that are borrowing in the money market. Only those companies that have no other choice will be willing to borrow on those terms. So as you shop for a money market fund, don't compare only the yields. Look at the funds' costs, too. It's virtually assured that the lower-cost fund is taking less risk with your money to achieve the same goal.

Getting back to the matter of bank certificates of deposit, here's a plan that will let you take advantage of higher rates from bank CDs yet still retain a healthy measure of liquidity. Once you've built up your emergency fund to whatever level you think is appropriate by investing in a money market fund, you can begin building what we'll call a "CD ladder," which is very similar to the "bond ladder" we'll discuss in the bond chapter. Let's say you have a cushion of $30,000 in your money market account. You could take $6,000 of that amount and buy a one-year CD (presuming the CD's yield is higher than your money market yield). That's the first "rung" of your CD ladder. Three months later take another $6,000 and buy another one-year CD. That's rung number two. See where we're going? At the end of the year you will have a four-rung CD ladder with $24,000 earning a higher rate than it did in your money market account. What's more, you'll never be more than three months away from being able to tap a total of $12,000—the $6,000 remaining in your money market account and a $6,000 CD maturing within three months. If you don't need the money from the CD, simply roll it over into another one-year CD.

THE PROCESS OF SAVING

It should become obvious after a few months of practicing tactical savings how much you bring home each week or month and how much you spend, on average, in the same time period. We'll hope the first is larger than the second. The difference between the two—your average weekly or monthly savings—should become the amount that is deflected periodically out of your spending account (your checking account) into your savings account.

One question that keeps recurring in my conversations with people wrestling their finances into some semblance of order is "How much should I have in savings?" My answer, unfortunately, is "It depends." I'm not copping out. I could give you the pat answer that many financial planners use: Have three months' (or six months', depending on the planner) salary in liquid savings. But that ignores what we're all trying to do: think about and control our finances. The real answer to how much you should have in savings depends on your own financial picture, your career, and your stage in life. A young single woman with a promising career needn't worry too much about being unemployed for a long time since she can probably get another job easily. Yet at the same time she probably hasn't accumulated much of an investment portfolio. She might be comfortable with three months or less in the bank. A professional administrator in his fifties might find it hard to get another job paying as well should he be "downsized" in a corporate restructuring. Yet he might also have a few hundred thousand dollars in his investment accounts that he could tap if and when he lost his job. He might be comfortable with three months' worth of savings, too. But take a working couple with three kids, one of whom is about to start college, and the circumstances are quite different. Not only does that couple need enough savings to cover the possible loss of a job for some period of time, they also need a bundle to meet looming college expenses. They would want at least a year's salary and maybe more at close hand. So study your own finances (that will be much easier when you know how much is coming in and how much is going out) and *think* about how you would cope with various scenarios.

In any event, if you don't have enough savings to be comfortable, you should divert money from your spending account to your savings account at a fairly high rate (think of it as filling the pipeline) before undertaking regular (and regularly increasing) investments in whatever long-term plan you devise. Once the pipeline is full, then shift most or all of the new money accumulating in your account books to your investment program. As you well know, your financial circumstances will change during the course of your life, and you will occasionally want—or need—to adjust the balance between savings and investing. But again, your knowledge of how money is flowing through your life should allow you to do that with a minimum amount of stress and strain.

TORY'S PORTFOLIOS: STOKING INVESTMENT PERFORMANCE WITH SAVINGS

It's unusual for an investment book to harp on savings as I've been doing in this chapter. Yet I firmly believe few people realize the amazing effects of adding new money to an investment portfolio. So let's wind up this discussion of savings with a concrete example of how saving can supercharge an investment program.

Meet Tory. She's a thirty-year-old employee of a Des Moines advertising firm, where she's worked since college graduation. For the sake of simplicity we'll assume that through company contributions to her 401(k) plan Tory has amassed a portfolio worth $10,000, all of it invested in a stock market index fund that has annual returns of 10.6 percent. And because her money is in a tax-advantaged retirement plan, Tory doesn't have to worry about the IRS taking a bite out of her gains each year. Unfortunately for the advertising agency, Tory is soon leaving to start a family, but she will leave her 401(k) plan invested in the stock fund. If nothing changes, here's what happens to that $10,000. Seven years from now it will have more than doubled in value to $20,244, which isn't bad. But as time passes, the effect of compounding—earlier earnings earning yet more earnings—begins to show up in increasingly dramatic fashion. At fourteen years the portfolio has more than doubled again, to $40,980, and it will keep doubling every seven years. (It's easy to figure out how frequently an investment will double in value: divide the number 72 by the percentage rate of return; in this case, 72/10.6 = 7.) Thirty years after she left work, and when she becomes eligible to start tapping those retirement funds, her portfolio will be worth twenty times the original investment, a total of $205,425. Should she choose to let it compound for another ten years until she's seventy, the account that started at $10,000 will be worth $562,607.

You can see in the table "Compound Returns on a Single

Sum" a graphic representation of what happens as the effects of compounding build over time:

COMPOUND RETURNS ON A SINGLE SUM

End of Year	Original Investment	Simple Earnings	Compound Earnings*	Total
1	$10,000	$ 1,060	—	$ 11,060
2	No change	$ 2,120	$ 112	$ 12,232
3	No change	$ 3,180	$ 349	$ 13,529
4	No change	$ 4,240	$ 723	$ 14,963
5	No change	$ 5,300	$ 1,249	$ 16,549
6	No change	$ 6,360	$ 1,943	$ 18,303
7	No change	$ 7,420	$ 2,824	$ 20,244
8	No change	$ 8,480	$ 3,909	$ 22,389
9	No change	$ 9,540	$ 5,223	$ 24,763
10	No change	$10,600	$ 6,787	$ 27,387
11	No change	$11,660	$ 8,630	$ 30,290
12	No change	$12,720	$ 10,781	$ 33,501
13	No change	$13,780	$ 13,272	$ 37,052
14	No change	$14,840	$ 16,140	$ 40,980
15	No change	$15,900	$ 19,424	$ 45,324
16	No change	$16,960	$ 23,168	$ 50,128
17	No change	$18,020	$ 27,422	$ 55,442
18	No change	$19,080	$ 32,239	$ 61,319
19	No change	$20,140	$ 37,678	$ 67,818
20	No change	$21,200	$ 43,807	$ 75,007
21	No change	$22,260	$ 50,698	$ 82,958
22	No change	$23,320	$ 58,431	$ 91,751
23	No change	$24,380	$ 67,097	$101,477
24	No change	$25,440	$ 76,794	$112,234
25	No change	$26,500	$ 87,630	$124,130
26	No change	$27,560	$ 99,728	$137,288
27	No change	$28,620	$113,221	$151,841
28	No change	$29,680	$128,256	$167,936
29	No change	$30,740	$144,997	$185,737
30	No change	$31,800	$163,625	$205,425
31	No change	$32,860	$184,340	$227,200
32	No change	$33,920	$207,364	$251,281
33	No change	$34,980	$232,940	$277,920
34	No change	$36,040	$261,339	$307,379
35	No change	$37,100	$292,861	$339,961
36	No change	$38,160	$327,837	$375,997
37	No change	$39,220	$366,633	$415,853
38	No change	$40,280	$409,653	$459,933
39	No change	$41,340	$457,346	$508,686
40	No change	$42,400	$510,207	$562,607

* *Earnings on earlier earnings.*

There are a few things about this chart that are especially interesting. Note that while the simple earnings accumulate relentlessly at the rate of $1,060 per year, the accumulated earnings on those earnings—the compound earnings—run along fairly flat for the first few years, begin to lift off, and finally zoom upward like a jet fighter taking off, then soar into the stratosphere. In the fourteenth year accumulated compound earnings overtake accumulated simple earnings. In the last year of this portfolio the compound earnings are growing at a rate of more than $50,000 per year. If ever there was an illustration that should prompt you to begin investing as early in life as possible, this is it.

While the effects of compounding alone are amazing, everything becomes much more interesting when compounding gains that important ally: new money. By new money I mean more money that is added to the portfolio on top of the initial investment and what it earns. Building on Tory's portfolio, let's change some circumstances and see what happens.

We'll say Tory decided not to start that family right away and kept working for the ad agency. And we'll assume the ad agency continued to make a $1,200 annual contribution to her 401(k) plan, which remained invested in the stock fund earning 10.6 percent annually. Just to be sure we're clear on what's happening, the table "Compound Returns on Modestly Increasing Investments" shows the activity in Tory's account in the first few years.

COMPOUND RETURNS ON MODESTLY INCREASING INVESTMENTS

End of Year	Initial Investment	New Money	Simple Earnings	Compound Earnings	Total
1	$10,000	$1,200	$1,187	—	$12,387
2	No change	$2,400	$2,502	$ 126	$15,028
3	No change	$3,600	$3,943	$ 404	$17,947
4	No change	$4,800	$5,512	$ 865	$21,177
5	No change	$6,000	$7,208	$1,541	$24,749

Recall how in our first example, where no new money was added, the simple earnings grew at a set pace of $1,060 a year? Look what's happening now. With each dollop of new money, Tory's simple earnings are growing by ever-increasing increments. While she receives $1,187 in simple earnings in the first year, by the fifth year simple earnings are producing $1,696. As with our first example, compound earnings are still loafing along, somewhat akin to that jet fighter taxiing out to the runway prior to take-off. But let's look further ahead. At ten years Tory's initial $10,000 stake and the $12,000 more that the ad agency has contributed to her retirement plan have together earned $17,596 in simple earn-ings. And the compound earnings—earnings on money earned earlier—total $9,562. Altogether her portfolio is worth $49,158. In our original example, when Tory had quit working, it took sixteen years for the portfolio to hit approximately that same level.

Jump ahead another ten years. It is now twenty years since Tory had that $10,000 stake. Since then her employer has faith-fully contributed $1,200 a year, for a total $24,000 on top of the original $10,000. That total investment of $34,000 has brought in $47,912 in simple earnings, while compound earnings total $74,489 (that jet has taken off), bringing her account balance to a very tidy $156,401. Under the original scenario it took nearly twenty-seven years to reach approximately that same level.

Now the jet's afterburners kick in and Tory's portfolio is zooming. At thirty years the total value is $450,112 (it took thirty-eight years to get there in the original example), and at forty years it is worth an astounding $1,254,513. That's $691,906 more than Tory would have had if there hadn't been any additions of new money to that original $10,000, and it's all the result of adding a rather modest sum—the equivalent of $100 a month—and com-pounding it for forty years.

Let's take this latest example a little further and suppose that along with her employer's contributions Tory decided to make vol-untary contributions to her 401(k) as well. We'll look only at the difference her contributions make to the results of her portfolio without complicating things by calculating how much she saves in income taxes by diverting some of her salary to the tax-advantaged plan. We'll assume she can match her employer's con-tribution of $1,200 each year. The table "Compound Returns on Larger Periodic Investments" shows what happens in the early years.

COMPOUND RETURNS ON LARGER PERIODIC INVESTMENTS

End of Year	Initial Investment	New Money	Simple Earnings	Compound Earnings	Total
1	$10,000	$ 2,400	$1,314	–	$13,714
2	No change	$ 4,800	$2,883	$ 139	$17,822
3	No change	$ 7,200	$4,706	$ 460	$22,366
4	No change	$ 9,600	$6,784	$1,007	$27,391
5	No change	$12,000	$9,116	$1,833	$32,949

Now simple earnings are growing a little faster each year as the additional new money provides more fuel. Compound earnings continue to grow slowly, but at the end of five years the overall portfolio is $8,200 larger than it would be if Tory wasn't contributing any of her own money. Now fast-forward to the tenth year. The original $10,000 stake has been supplemented by a total of $24,000 of new money contributed by Tory and her employer. The simple interest totals $24,592, and the compound interest amounts to $12,336 (the jet is lifting off the runway), for a grand total of $70,928. It would have taken Tory thirteen years to reach that if she hadn't been contributing her money, and nearly twenty years to hit that goal if her original $10,000 stake had been left to grow unaided. After twenty years of adding $2,400 annually to the portfolio, it looks like this: The original $10,000 has been joined by another $48,000 of contributions. That total has earned $74,624 in simple returns; but the compound returns total $105,171 (the jet is climbing now), bringing Tory's portfolio to $237,795. At thirty years the portfolio totals $694,800, setting the stage once again for the power of compounding to assert itself forcefully. In the final ten years the portfolio nearly trebles to $1,946,418, including $1,589,410 of compound earnings (the afterburner is on again) and $251,008 of simple earnings. The total amount invested? Just $106,000.

What we've examined so far has been the effect on a portfolio of compounding a fixed amount of money and then adding a fixed amount of money to a base amount. I want to construct one final portfolio in this discussion of compounding and adding money to a portfolio to demonstrate what I believe is the most desirable scenario: adding increasing amounts of money to a portfolio each year. It's hard to say that there is a typical career anymore, but for the sake of this illustration we'll presume that an individual investor has a job that produces annual raises (some large, some small) and occasional bonuses. We'll assume, too, that some of that additional money is eaten up by the costs of housing, by having and educating kids, and by indulging oneself in hobbies or sports. But we'll also assume that expenses fall later in life. The net result of all these assumptions, we'll say, is that the typical investor should be able to find an additional 5 percent each year on average to contribute to his or her investment program. To keep this simple, we'll assume the additional amount goes into a tax-advantaged retirement plan (we'll deal with the effects of taxes and other drains on investment returns later in the book).

Back to Tory at age thirty. She has her $10,000, her employer is contributing $1,200 a year to her 401(k), and so is she. But as her income rises, her employer's contributions to her 401(k) rise, too, and she kicks in more of her own money each year. The net result is that the amount of new money flowing into Tory's portfolio grows by 5 percent per year. The early returns are shown in the table "Compound Returns on Increasing Amounts Invested."

COMPOUND RETURNS ON INCREASING AMOUNTS INVESTED

End of Year	Initial Investment	New Money	Simple Earnings	Compound Earnings	Total
1	$10,000	$ 2,400	$1,314	—	$13,714
2	No change	$ 4,920	$2,896	$ 139	$17,955
3	No change	$ 7,566	$4,758	$ 461	$22,785
4	No change	$10,344	$6,914	$1,014	$28,272
5	No change	$13,262	$9,380	$1,855	$34,497

By increasing the amount of each year's contributions, Tory and her employer are, in effect, compounding the new money that is coming into the portfolio at the rate of 5 percent per year. You'll notice if you do the math that new money in the second year is $120 more than it was in the earlier example, when the new money flowing into the portfolio was fixed at $2,400. Well, 5 percent of $2,400 is $120. As we've seen in the earlier examples, the power of compounding takes a while to work its wonders. And that's true when you're compounding new money just as it is when you're compounding earnings. At the end of five years this portfolio is only $1,548 ahead of the portfolio that was based on the fixed amount of $2,400 of new money each year. Hardly impressive, is it?

But you know what's coming next: we're jumping ahead now to demonstrate the long-term compounding effects of a paltry 5 percent increase in each year's new money flowing into the portfolio. At ten years we find that $30,187 of new money has been invested in Tory's portfolio compared with $24,000 in the fixed contribution portfolio. Simple earnings in the new portfolio total $26,916 and compound earnings are $12,891, for a total portfolio value of $79,994. In the fixed contribution portfolio, the ten-year total was $70,928. At year twenty new money invested has climbed to $79,358 compared with $48,000 in the fixed contribution portfolio. The total portfolio has benefited, too, from increasing compound earnings (they totaled $119,325 in year twenty) for a total portfolio value of $304,775, or $66,980 more than the fixed-contribution portfolio. At year thirty the increasing contributions produce a total portfolio value of $974,281 compared with $694,800 in the fixed-contribution account. And—drumroll here—in the fortieth year the grand total of Tory's portfolio has climbed to $2,895,668, a stunning $949,250 more than if she and the ad agency had continued to contribute just the $2,400 each year. The total amount of new money invested was $289,919, or $193,919 more than in the fixed plan.

The amounts that we've talked about sound fantastic to many people. But the fact is that the assumptions I've used in these examples are not at all extreme. Someone who takes full advantage of a retirement plan, invests the money in stocks, and continues to work past age sixty-five can expect to equal or even surpass these figures. If you don't think you want to work past age sixty, simply use the thirty-year results as an approximation of what you might have in a retirement account at age sixty. Of course, everyone's results will vary to some extent, depending upon individual circumstances. But keep in mind that our discussion has centered on a simple retirement plan (to which contributions are limited by law). Should you also set up an investment program outside of your retirement plan—if you bought this book, you're probably already thinking about or are in the middle of doing just that—then the amount of money available to you years from now could be substantially larger, despite the fact that you'll have to contend with the burden of taxes on some of your gains.

And that's what the rest of this book is about.

2

STOCKS:

The Foundation
of a Strong Portfolio

YOU PROBABLY KNOW ALL ABOUT DEFAULT SETTINGS: when you crank up your computer, the default setting is where it goes automatically. You can switch to some other program or type size or font or screen color if you wish. But you have to actively make the switch to another setting. Stocks should be the default setting of your investment portfolio. Unless you have a reason to seek out some other kind of investment, any money you're investing should go automatically to stocks. There will certainly be occasions on which you choose not to go to stocks. You may select cash to meet bills coming due soon or bonds to lock in a safe and predictable return leading up to the first college tuition payment ten years from now. But absent an obvious reason for choosing something else, stocks should be your preference for the same reason Willie Sutton robbed banks: That's where the money is.

Experts are still debating exactly what the long-term rate of return is for stocks. As you might expect, records from before the turn of the century—the last century, not the new one that just arrived—aren't always precise. Based on the best available data and the opinions of experts I respect, I'll settle for 12 percent as the average annual return for a portfolio of U.S. stocks for the period 1926 to 1997. But while the exact number may be in dispute, the point is conceded by all: No readily available asset—cash, real estate, and bonds are other broad classifications—has performed as well over the years as a portfolio of common stocks. Not every year. Not even every five years. But studies examining investment returns have shown that there are no ten-year periods in which stocks didn't do better than anything else, even in the lengthy depression that followed the Crash of 1929.

More than any other asset class, stocks reflect the dynamic growth and change that are occurring both within the United States, far and away the world's most powerful economy, and in the world at large. By owning a selected chunk of all the stocks available both here and abroad, the average investor can expect, over the long term, to obtain the best possible returns on his or her money consistent with taking a reasonable risk.

Notice I said "reasonable risk." Make no mistake, stocks carry a certain amount of risk. We'll get into specific ways to define risk and to identify risks surrounding both individual stocks and the stock market as a whole. But for the moment, I'll just say that risk is the chance that you won't get the kind of return you were seeking when you bought your stock portfolio. When you consider that 12 percent average annual return, remember that it is only an average that conceals some truly vast swings in values. Had you bought a portfolio of stocks at the beginning of 1931, for instance, it would have been down more than 43 percent in value at the end of that year. Conversely, a portfolio assembled on the first business day of 1933 would have been worth nearly 54 percent more just a year later. Those are the worst- and best-case instances (so far, at least) for *portfolios*. They don't address what can happen to individual stocks. Some recently issued stocks in Internet-related companies have more than tripled on their first day of trading, and a doubling in value over a period of a just a year or two is common enough in the stock market that nobody even comments on it. Yet a disconcertingly large number of companies, along with their stocks, simply disappear from the face of the earth each year, the result of the many business failures that occur in the fiercely competitive U.S. economy.

Time, though, does have a knack of at least partially healing investment wounds (it also tempers investment euphoria by paring away at those incredibly high returns of the best years). Consider what happens if you assume that an investor bought a portfolio of stocks on a given day since 1926 and held that portfolio for five years. The worst our long-term investor would have suffered was a 12.5 percent average annual loss. Certainly that wouldn't have been pleasant, but it wouldn't have been a disaster like that 43 percent loss in 1931. The best that would have befallen our investor would have been a 23.9 percent average annual gain, hardly the grand return of 54 percent in 1933 but well over twice the average annual return for a stock portfolio. Now assume a holding period of twenty years. The worst situation confronting an investor was a 3.1 percent average annual *gain*—that's right, a gain—about the same as one would realize by holding cash in an interest-bearing bank account. The best average annual gain, however, would have been pared to 16.9 percent, which in historical perspective is still very impressive. These kinds of returns illustrate why I will warn you several times in this book that stocks are for long-term investment portfolios and can be dangerous weapons when used for short-term investment ("speculation" might be the better term).

I realize that compared with a 50 percent or more annual gain, or even to the 20 percent–plus gains that the market enjoyed in the last half of the 1990s, 12 percent sounds puny. But lest you sneer at such returns, let's compare what happens to an all-stock portfolio when placed against a common alternative portfolio that is essentially riskless: long-term U.S. government bonds. We'll start with $10,000 and examine two holding periods: five years and twenty years. The table "Comparative Returns of Stocks and Bonds" shows the results.

COMPARATIVE RETURNS OF STOCKS AND BONDS

	Start	5 Years	20 Years
All stocks (12% average annual gain)	$10,000	$17,623	$96,463
All long-term gov.'t bonds (5% average annual gain)	$10,000	$12,760	$26,530

I know the so-called financial experts will criticize my heavy emphasis on stocks. They'll argue that most people should have a portfolio more evenly balanced between stocks and much less volatile bonds. Part of their reasoning is perfectly valid: Some people simply can't stand the psychological pressure of seeing their portfolio fall 20 percent or more in a short time, and that will almost certainly occur—probably more than once—during any normal investor's lifetime. If you're one of those people—and only you know if you are—then certainly tempering your portfolio with bonds is a worthwhile endeavor. But another reason professional investment advisers argue for a more balanced portfolio is that investors almost always blame the advisers when portfolio values drop, and the advisers get very tired of that. Recommending a balanced portfolio gets them off the hook to some extent. The argument for a balanced portfolio is that you reduce the riskiness—the volatility—of the portfolio. But my counterargument is that if you start investing in stocks early enough and plan carefully for what you'll need in the future, an all-stock portfolio will give you a sizable cushion even in times of market tumult. Here's a simple explanation of what I mean:

Let's assume you have a twenty-five-year investment horizon and at the end of that time you want a portfolio that will provide you with $80,000 annually on which to live. At 6 percent, the yield you might expect from Treasury bonds, you'll need $1,334,000 twenty-five years from now. To get to that amount at 6 percent per year (forget, for the moment, taxes on the income from your bonds each year), you'll need to save $23,000 per year. If instead you saved $23,000 a year in stocks providing an average 10 percent per year, you would have at the end of twenty-five years a portfolio worth nearly $2.5 million, which on average could provide you with $250,000 in income in any given year. Since you need only $80,000 (no fair raising your standard of living to *require* all $250,000), you would have an enormous cushion to withstand some really violent financial storms.

Now do you see why I make stocks the default setting on any long-term investment portfolio? Certainly there are risks, but the kinds of returns made over the long haul are well worth those risks.

REALITY CHECK!

Before you dive headlong into stock investing, however, I have a small confession to make: While I would love it if you were enormously successful as a stock investor, I suspect you probably won't make 12 percent annually on your own portfolio of stocks. Besides the enormous hurdle of picking the right stocks—I'll have a lot more to say on that subject in the rest of this chapter—you will face two smaller hurdles that don't affect market measures like the Dow Jones Industrial Average or Standard & Poor's 500 stock index: transaction costs and taxes. The calculations that lead to the conclusion that stocks return an average of 12 percent annually assume that the stocks can be bought and sold free. In the real world of greedy brokers and frowning IRS agents, that isn't possible. When you buy or sell a stock, there's a cost attached to it. It may not be much—perhaps as little as $8 per trade through some Internet stock services—but it lowers your return. And then you have to give part of your winnings—how big a part depends on your income—to your friends at the Internal Revenue Service. If you picked a hot stock and made a killing in less than twelve months, you could wind up giving back nearly 40 percent of your gains to the government as ordinary income taxes. If you were more conservative and made that killing in thirteen months and thus became eligible for long-term capital gains treatment of your profits, your maximum contribution to running the government would be 20 percent of the gain. But in either case you're watching your performance shrink sharply against that 12 percent return you thought you could count on.

Tough.

Just keep in mind that with alternative investments you're almost always worse off. If you opt for Treasury bonds and their much lower average annual gains, you'll be paying ordinary income taxes on every interest check you get. If you choose tax-free municipal bonds, you can escape the tax burden, but only at the price of higher risk and lower interest payments (for some high-tax-bracket investors, the yield on muni bonds can exceed that of Treasury bonds but still comes nowhere near matching the performance of stocks).

All this is just to say at the outset that you shouldn't set your expectations too high. That way lies disappointment, and it would be a costly shame if you became disenchanted with stocks just because you weren't earning 20 percent per year, or even 12 percent per year. Just remember that almost everything else you might invest in will return even less.

How to Think About Stocks and the Stock Market

In my years of watching the stock market gyrate (and trying to explain those gyrations on a daily basis), I have noticed a curious phenomenon that tends to be more common among amateur investors but can afflict the pros as well. In their frenzy to make huge profits, or to avoid huge losses, investors sometimes seem to lose sight of the fact that stocks—and the markets in which they're traded—aren't stand-alone products. These investors talk and act as if Microsoft were nothing more than a word that represents a set of moves on a computer terminal or in the stock columns of their local newspaper. They hope the Microsoft number goes up, not down. They toss out names of stocks without knowing what the tiny companies that issued the stocks actually do. They seem to forget, or choose to ignore, that the stocks they are chasing so eagerly represent companies that do something. These companies offer products or services, compete with others that do the same thing, and either make a profit or lose money doing it. But to the investors who buy and sell the companies' stocks, it isn't a question of how well the company is doing, it's just a question of how well the stock is doing.

There's a place in the world for that kind of investor. Indeed, that approach to stock market investing reaches its apotheosis in a company with the unwieldy name of BNP/Cooper Neff Advisors, a small investment firm in Radnor, Pennsylvania. Each week BNP/Cooper Neff trades 100 million to 150 million shares of stock on the New York Stock Exchange, as much as 6 percent of the Big Board's weekly volume. And it does so without knowing anything about the companies behind those stocks. Cooper Neff traders don't know what a company does, they don't know who the chairman is, they don't know if it's making money or losing money. In fact, they don't even know the name of the company. Instead they rely on complex mathematical algorithms that are designed to remove all emotions from the purchase and sale of a stock.

Andrew Sterge, the young mathematical wizard who runs the firm, argues that it's a waste of time to try to determine what a share of stock in a company is worth. "There's no god who knows the fair value of any traded asset," he says. "The only way you can know anything about value is how the market tries to find an equilibrium. That's all the market is—a big feedback mechanism trying to find equilibrium." And the only way to beat the market, says Mr. Sterge, is to use computers to trade millions of shares of thousands of stocks in search of tiny inefficiencies. If the computer can be right slightly more than half the time, the huge volumes and narrow margins turn into fat profits.

But I'm assuming you don't have a computer that big, or the money to do that many trades each week, or the mathematical formulas that will let you capture slight price discrepancies. So if you want to own individual stocks, you're going to have to figure out some method of determining which ones to buy, when to buy them, and when to sell them. It seems fairly logical that the only way to do that is to know something about the company behind the stock. On Wall Street the research function aimed at knowing all about the companies behind the stock is called "securities analysis," and its practitioners are usually very smart, well educated, and highly paid. And they still don't get it right that often. In part that's because they're up against thousands of other very smart people all trying to do the same thing, and their collective judgment is at work every minute of the trading day. In effect, while they are as competitive as human beings can get and dearly love to outperform all their competitors, in reality they are all tacitly working together to set a price for each stock and for the stock market as a whole.

The Odds Against You: The Efficient Market Hypothesis

Before you embark on a concentrated effort to learn how to pick winning stocks, or at least before you go any further into the process if you've already started, I want to be sure you're going in with eyes wide open. That's why I want to acquaint you with the "efficient market hypothesis" (EMH). If you accept this hypothesis in its strictest form—that the market encapsulates all knowledge about the value of stocks—then you can willingly give up your quest to outsmart the market and devote all the time and effort that would have gone into researching individual stocks to something a lot more fun, like coaching soccer, playing golf, or catching fish. Granted, not everyone is convinced that the hypothesis is correct, at least in its strict form. Certainly Andrew Sterge at BNP/Cooper Neff would seem to be proof that some inefficiencies are there; if they weren't, there would be nothing for his computers and mathematical formulas to find, and the firm would go broke. To be sure, there are other, more lenient forms of the hypothesis that allow for some measure of individual stock-picking success. Finally, there are those who dismiss the hypothesis entirely, contending that by rigorous analysis and hard work an investor can outsmart the market. It is only with some reluctance that I have come to the conclusion that if the market isn't 100 percent efficient, it is still damned efficient. Taking that stance leaves me embarrassingly at odds with some very smart investors—smarter and more experienced than I am—for whom I have a great deal of respect. But it also leaves me with lots of time to do other things than chase stock market returns. And I still have an investment portfolio that is providing me with very pleasing results.

At the heart of the efficient market hypothesis is information. The hypothesis assumes that the vast body of investors will quickly absorb all available information about a stock and reflect that information in the price of the stock. The information includes what happened to the company and the stock in the past (earnings and stock performance in a recession, for example), what is happening currently (an unexpected change in top management that has just been announced), and what may reasonably be assumed will happen in the near future (if the Federal Reserve has embarked on a course of cutting interest rates, for example, that information will be reflected in a stock's price). No one person has all this information. Instead, each of thousands of investors has bits and pieces and acts accordingly. The sum of their actions is the sum of all the knowledge they have—the price of the stock. And the total impact of all that information need not be reflected instantly in a stock price. The price can adjust over a period of minutes, hours, or even days, as the data are absorbed and evaluated. But don't count on that lag to give you an upper hand. According to the hypothesis, during the time that information is being absorbed the stock price may fluctuate too high or too low—you don't know which—until it settles at a value reflective of all knowledge. Your chances of profiting or losing on the lag are fifty-

fifty (simply a random guess). The upshot of the efficient market hypothesis in its strictest form is that no single investor can obtain abnormally large profits by knowing something that other investors don't know.

Obviously the market is not perfectly efficient. The mania that surrounded the so-called dot-com stocks seems ample evidence of that. But how efficient is it? Adherents of the efficient market hypothesis have devised different ways to describe how efficient the market is that reflect their varying levels of confidence in the hypothesis. At the low end of confidence is the "weak form" of the hypothesis. This form maintains only that all past price and volume information of a stock is reflected in the current price of the stock. Thus knowledge of the past performance of the stock won't be of any use to an investor trying to gain an upper hand since that performance is already reflected in the price. This form of the EMH effectively knocks down the entire discipline known as "technical analysis," which utilizes charts and graphs of the past performance of a stock to predict its future performance.

The next step up in acknowledging the effectiveness of the EMH is the "semistrong form." This includes the weak form, which assumes that all previous price action is reflected in a stock price, and adds to it the assumption that all other current knowledge about a stock is in the price as well. This means that anything a company does that can be known by the public, from declaring a dividend to having a product recalled or firing an executive, is quickly reflected in the stock price. In the United States, where dissemination of information is especially swift and comprehensive, it seems likely that the market is certainly efficient in a semistrong sense. You might note that this form of the EMH seems to leave room for corporate insiders or especially diligent researchers to know and utilize for a profit certain aspects of a company that aren't known to the public at large. Obviously insiders might know about developments in the company that aren't yet public, but trading on that information is illegal and can cost them both heavy fines and time in jail. And certainly there are opportunities to dig deeply into a company to find information others don't have. But the EMH doesn't even let you get away with that. It simply argues that the additional profits such diligent research permits are, at best, large enough only to reimburse you for the cost of all that research.

The strictest sense of the EMH, the one with which we opened this discussion, is called the "strong form." It holds that all information, both public and private, is contained in a stock's price. While there are obviously money managers who outperform such well-known stock market measures as the Dow Jones Industrial Average and the S&P 500, the strict form of the EMH argues that they are simply statistical anomalies, their performance being similar to that of the coin flipper who turns up heads ten times in a row. It looks as though something besides chance is at work, but in reality the next flip has a fifty-fifty chance of being tails. Likewise, the EMH contends that a seemingly great money manager, even after outperforming the market for ten years in a row, could on any given day begin underperforming the market. In other words, the ability to outperform the market cannot be predicted in advance or sustained forever. Advocates of the EMH concede that there will surely be four or five mutual fund managers who will have produced stunning performances five years from now, far outpacing the market. But nobody can say today who they will be.

Regardless of your view on the EMH, here's a sobering thought to keep in mind: If you're smart enough to find an inefficiency—a stock that is priced too low for some reason—and act on that information, you have automatically helped make the market *more* efficient. The point is, if there are inefficiencies, somebody is going to find out about them. It may be Mr. Sterge's computers, or it may be one of the hundreds of thousands of individual investors who use the incredible resources available on the Internet to do their own stock research. In any event, if they do find an inefficiency, they immediately take advantage of it, effectively eliminating it. And that results in the inevitable conclusion that if markets aren't yet totally efficient, they're certainly moving in that direction.

With the efficient market hypothesis firmly in mind, let's look at the ways in which professional investment managers or brokers will try to sell you on their methods for beating the market. And their sales pitches can be persuasive. Their methods sound logical, and they'll certainly bolster that impression by recounting performance figures that show them soundly beating the overall market.

FINDING VALUE IN STOCKS

We'll start with a look at value investing, because, if markets *are* efficient, value investing doesn't work; it works only if they are *not* efficient. If you continue to delve deeper into stock investing, you may hear someone discussing Graham and Dodd. They're referring to the father of value investing, Benjamin Graham, and his chief disciple, David Dodd, who in 1934 coauthored the bible of the value investor, a weighty tome called *Security Analysis*. The book is available today in its fifth incarnation and contains a wealth of information about how to analyze and invest in stocks and bonds. At $59.95 it isn't cheap, and applying its lessons isn't easy. But short of taking a university-level course in financial analysis at considerably more expense, it's the single best resource for a determined value investor.

At the heart of the Graham and Dodd approach to stock investing is the determination of a company's intrinsic value: what the company is worth when its assets, earnings, dividends, outlook, and management are all taken into account. Determining the value of each of those factors and adding them up to arrive at a price for a share of a company's stock isn't nearly as easy as it may sound. Certain assumptions have to be made about the investment environment, management's capabilities, and the value of assets. And once the intrinsic value is determined, it changes, albeit slowly, because companies are doing business in a competitive and ever-changing environment. Nevertheless, it still remains the goal of the best securities analysts to determine the intrinsic value of a company.

Once the intrinsic value is determined, it is then compared to the company's stock price and a judgment is made. If the investor doesn't own the stock, the decision is whether to avoid it or buy it. If the intrinsic value is far above the stock price, the decision would be to buy it and wait for other investors to discover what you have (market efficiency at work) and bid the stock price up closer to the intrinsic value. If the investor owns the stock, then the decision is whether to hold it or sell it. If the stock price is still below the intrinsic value, you would hold. If the stock price is close to or above the intrinsic value, you would sell before other investors discover what you have and bid the stock price down to the intrinsic value. The interesting thing about adherents to the Graham and Dodd approach is that they want—indeed, must have—a reasonably efficient market or there is no point to their exercise of determining intrinsic value. But they cannot have a 100 percent efficient market, because that would mean that a company's intrinsic value and its stock price would always be the same, leaving no room to make profits based on all that analysis. Instead, value investors argue that stock prices, responding to a variety of factors (not the least of which is investors' volatile emotions), move both above and below intrinsic value, coinciding with it only occasionally, but usually trending toward it. In other words, they assume that if a stock price is higher than the intrinsic value, the stock price eventually will fall closer to that value. If the stock price is below intrinsic value, it eventually will move higher. To make money, an investor buys a stock when its price is below the intrinsic value of the company and sells it when it is at or above intrinsic value. One can also make money, although at substantially more risk, by borrowing shares of a stock whose price is above the intrinsic value and promptly selling those shares, then buying them back and returning them to their original owner when the stock price falls below intrinsic value, a process called "short selling."

Sounds pretty simple, doesn't it? All you have to do to get rich is start calculating the intrinsic values of bunches of companies, then buy the stocks of companies whose share price is below their intrinsic value. But, of course, you know that if it were that easy, everybody would be doing it. And if everybody did it, they would already have bought up all the stocks trading at less than the intrinsic value of the companies that issued the stock. The market would have become 100 percent efficient, or very close to it. As I said, using the Graham and Dodd method to calculate intrinsic value is itself a complicated process, and it is possible to get the wrong answer. If you're working with the wrong answer and another investor has the right answer, you're going to lose money. But there's another problem, and it relates to the point I made a moment ago, about everybody else doing the same thing: To calculate an accurate intrinsic value for a company, that company has to have been around long enough to have compiled a reasonably long series of earnings and price movements. Many such companies have grown so large that they've attracted lots of attention from Wall Street. In short, the kinds of companies that are most susceptible to this kind of analysis are already being analyzed to a fare-thee-well. Do you think those highly paid men and women on Wall Street are going to let you discover something they missed? If they do, they won't be highly paid analysts on Wall Street for very long.

That isn't to say that value stocks are impossible to find, at least if Graham and Dodd are correct in assuming that stock prices react to things like investor emotion. There are times, for example, in which investors in large numbers become fearful of owning stocks and seem to sell somewhat irrationally. The stock market crash of 1987, *in hindsight*, was one such period. An alert investor—and one with the courage of his or her convictions— would have done very well by buying a broad range of big, well-known stocks in the immediate aftermath of that stunning fall. But it isn't easy to be courageous in such circumstances. We recognized only long after the event that the 1987 crash was a temporary disruption. At the time some very smart people—including Alan Greenspan, who had only recently been appointed to head the Federal Reserve—thought it signaled the beginning of tremendous stress on the U.S. economy. Conversely, more than a few investors regarded the Great Crash of 1929 as a temporary setback. They suffered the consequences of that misjudgment for more than a decade.

If someone can predict accurately what the economy is going to do (I don't know anyone who can do that on a sustained basis), value investing offers some opportunities to make money through the subdiscipline of investing in cyclical issues. Certain industries, ranging from steel to automobiles to financial services, tend to track the ups and downs of the business cycle. An expanding economy creates demand for cars; the demand for cars in turn creates demand for steel. As the automakers and steel mills increase production, they make better use of their expensive factories and their profit outlook improves. And, of course, an improving profit outlook tends to bring with it an improving stock price. Similarly, financial services companies—which use money as their raw material—tend to enjoy higher profits as the cost of money (interest rates) goes down and to be less profitable when interest rates go up. The trouble is, predicting the course of the economy and interest rates isn't simple. Get it wrong and you either buy cyclical stocks too late or hang on to them too long.

When the market isn't in wholesale retreat, value investing becomes very difficult. By its nature, value investing often involves investing in distressed companies. If they weren't distressed, they wouldn't be selling cheaply. The value investor's hope is that a company can overcome whatever is causing the distress and rally back to health, taking its stock price with it. But there is a chance that it won't recover, that whatever is causing the problems that have brought the stock price low will ultimately be fatal and the stock price will go to zero. That's one reason some of the most effective value investors tend to prefer large companies: it's simply much harder to kill a huge company than a small one. Nevertheless a dedicated value investor will shop among the smaller-capitalization stocks in search of potential targets. It is more difficult to determine an intrinsic value for small or recently formed companies, but the lack of competition from every Tom, Dick, and Harriet analyst on Wall Street at least affords an opportunity to find something interesting.

Different value investors use different ways to identify a possible stock to add to their portfolio. One of the most popular tools, one that individuals can use fairly easily, is the price-to-earnings ratio. The P/E ratio is merely the price per share of stock divided by the annual earnings per share the company reported (trailing) or is expected to report (projected). Generally a P/E of 10 or less on trailing twelve months' earnings suggests that value investors should at least do some further analysis of the company. But they must do that work before they buy: there often is a fine reason that the P/E ratio is low, and it's likely to go lower.

When professional investors do find a company with a low P/E ratio that they feel is being unfairly penalized by the market, they still don't necessarily buy the stock. Rather, they ask a basic question: If this stock is undervalued, how long and what will it take for all the other investors out there to realize it and bid up the price so I can make a profit? If there isn't a clear answer, the stock might not make it into the investor's portfolio. But if there is a catalyst, something looming that will bring the stock to the attention of other investors—a management shake-up, perhaps, or a new and improved version of the company's product—then it becomes a much more likely pick.

Yet for all their rational discipline, value investors have had a very tough time over the last decade or so. They argue that value stocks haven't been "in style" amid the frenzy over fast-growing technology and Internet stocks. Efficient market advocates, of course, argue that market pricing is cyclical and that sick company stocks are exactly where they should be priced given what is known about them. Certainly some of those companies and their stocks will do very well. But others won't, and the trouble is, nobody knows in advance which ones will and which ones won't. Meanwhile the overall market just keeps marching higher, leaving the value investors, diligently studying Graham and Dodd, in its wake.

GROWTH STOCKS: HOW HIGH, HOW FAST?

Don't ask a growth stock investor to calculate the intrinsic value of a company. She doesn't care. Ask her how fast earnings are growing, though, and she can tell you the percentage gains in each of the last eight or so quarters and give you projections on the eight quarters yet to come. Earnings—specifically earnings growth—are the heart of growth stock investing. Earnings are growing fast? The stock will rise fast. Earnings in a slump? The stock is going down. A stock with a price/earnings ratio of 60, a level that would give a value investor a heart attack, doesn't even faze your average growth investor if he or she figures it can go to 80. At its best, growth stock investing will get you into the next Microsoft long before most people have even heard the company's name for the first time. At its worst, you can lose an awful lot of money awfully fast. At its best, growth investing will take you into the most exciting parts of the economy—technology, the Internet, health care, or retailing, for example—where big, sophisticated, and innovative companies are talked about in awed tones and new companies with surprising products or new services are springing up constantly. At its worst, it will lead you into the realm of the greater fool, a place where you buy a stock at a ridiculously high price on the presumption that someone even dumber than you will buy it from you at an even more ridiculous price.

Two concepts are central to almost every growth investor's analysis of a stock: the rate of earnings growth and the multiple the stock can command. The rate of earnings growth can be understood to mean two things. First, it can be the average pace at which earnings per share for a given company are growing. There is no set definition of what constitutes a growth stock, but many of the best and brightest money managers who follow this discipline focus on companies that are posting 20-percent-per-year increases in their per-share earnings. Now, 20 percent doesn't sound like such a huge number. But consider that at a rate of 20 percent per year a company's earnings will more than double in just four years. A small company growing at such a furious pace will almost certainly encounter some sort of stumbling block: managing the expansion of factories, for example, or hiring and keeping quality employees (including managers). And a large company will face the monumental challenge of finding an ever-increasing supply of new customers and markets to conquer to maintain a 20-percent-per-year growth rate. Neither the small nor the large company will find its goals easy to meet year after year. A disappointment over a quarter or an entire year will sadly disillusion investors, who almost certainly paid a premium price to obtain a premium growth rate. Absent the premium growth rate, they will quickly bring the price down to something more appropriate.

The second definition of earnings growth involves acceleration. Investors looking for this kind of company want to see the *rate* of earnings growth rising in each quarter or year. They're looking for a company whose earnings grew 5 percent in the second quarter over the first quarter, 10 percent in the third quarter over the second quarter, and 20 percent in the fourth quarter over the third quarter. In short, they're looking for a company whose earnings profile, laid out on a piece of graph paper, looks like the flight profile of a jet fighter going down the runway, then climbing swiftly into the stratosphere. Needless to say, mathematics suggests that growth rates that are accelerating at that kind of pace cannot be sustained for long. When they begin to slacken, as they inevitably must, the stock price follows a pattern closely akin to a jet plane that runs out of fuel at fifty thousand feet. This subspecialty of growth stock investing is known as "momentum investing." It isn't a game for the faint of heart, and because it requires extremely close attention to a company's business—virtually day-to-day monitoring—it isn't something most individuals should attempt.

Many growth investors use the price-earnings multiple a stock commands as a tool roughly equivalent to the value investor's intrinsic value, a way to measure a stock price against a benchmark. For example, a growth investor might compare the price-earnings multiple of one semiconductor maker against the P/Es of other semiconductor makers to help determine if the stock is desirable. If the P/E of the stock is the same as that of the average semiconductor maker and its earnings growth rate is about in line with that of the rest of the industry, there would not be a compelling reason to buy the stock. But if the P/E were the same as the average semiconductor maker's and the company's earnings were growing faster, then a case could be made that the market will eventually assign a higher P/E to the stock, allowing room for the stock price to rise.

Not surprisingly, semiconductor stocks probably will have an average P/E that is very much higher than the P/E of the average steel company, simply because the growth rates in those industries are very different. The prize that many growth investors seek is a company that is in transition, shifting its business from one that is valued at a low P/E multiple to one that is valued at a high P/E multiple. A (very) hypothetical example would be a steel company that has found a way to use its blast furnaces to make semiconductor chips. As news of the discovery leaks out, growth investors will suddenly decide that the company's earnings now will grow at a rate similar to that of other semiconductor makers rather than at the rate of other steelmakers. Presto! The stock price can now rise tenfold and still be a good buy, because earnings growth expectations have suddenly risen.

Such stories aren't common, but they do occur in more modest circumstances. One popular example occurred at the dawn of the personal computer era, when Tandy Corp., which operated Radio Shack stores around the country, introduced its own personal computer. Suddenly the stock went from being valued as a retailer to being valued as a technology company. The lucky investors who had bought it when it was thought to be a retailer got rich. Later investors, who bought it when it was valued as a technology company, didn't do so well, finding out the hard way that technology is a ruthlessly competitive business that changes almost day to day. Tandy, now renamed Radio Shack, is back to being valued as a retailer.

None of this is to suggest that investors can't make money buying growth stocks. To the contrary, growth stock investing can be immensely rewarding. Just ask anyone who bought Microsoft or Wal-Mart ten years ago or Coca-Cola twenty years ago. The returns on those stocks have far exceeded those of the overall market. But I suspect that those same investors, aiming to diversify their portfolios, also bought lots of other growth stocks at the same time that haven't grown as fast or become as large as Microsoft, Wal-Mart, or Coca-Cola. And the money they've lost by betting on that growth has probably brought their average return over the last ten or twenty years pretty close to the market's average. Add in the costs of trading and the taxes they paid on gains, and they may even be below the market's average return.

Discussions with professional money managers and analysts who pursue a growth strategy suggest to me that growth investing lends itself more easily than value investing to what, for lack of a better term, I'll call "story investing." This approach simply calls for an investor to consider the story behind a company. The point, as one money manager puts it, is "to find a company that is so exciting, it will capture the imagination of other investors." Most recently the story du jour was the Internet. Any company that made a plausible claim to have business on or from the World Wide Web was instantly treated as having virtually unlimited growth potential. Amazon.com, the Internet-based bookseller, was an early beneficiary of this particular story, and its stock rose so far and so fast that it was beyond the comprehension of many Wall Street professionals.

Some earlier story stocks have proven their worth over the years and even spawned variations on their basic themes that have also proved profitable for investors. A case in point is Home Depot, the amazingly successful hardware and building supply retailer that brought the "big box" concept—a large store with a focus on a specific business that does sufficient volume to keep prices low—to the fore. Home Depot created a nationwide network of large, well-staffed, and well-stocked hardware and building supply stores. Staples did the same thing for the office supply business. But there have been abject failures of story stocks, too. The biotech industry, which basically aims to create new drugs targeted at anything from curing cancer or AIDS to lowering blood pressure, is littered with stories about promising drugs that, when subjected to rigorous testing, failed to live up to their earlier promises, much to the regret and financial loss of many investors.

Of course, at any given moment you will not be the only investor out there looking at the earnings growth rates and considering the stories behind a typical growth stock. Under just about any form of the efficient market hypothesis that I discussed early in this chapter, the prices of the stocks you're looking at will reflect to a great extent the combined judgments of all those other investors, leaving you in the same fix you were in when you considered value stocks: finding the few stocks that will be real winners while avoiding those that will be losers.

NARROWING THE FIELD: MARKET CAPITALIZATION

Value and growth investing are the two broadest methods by which professional investors describe their approach to stock picking. To further narrow the range of stocks from which they choose their portfolio components, many pros classify their styles by the size of the stocks they research. Size, in this case, refers to the market capitalization of a company, which is merely the per-share price multiplied by the number of shares outstanding. If, for example, a company has 100 million shares outstanding (that is, it has at some time in the past sold 100 million shares to the investing public) and those shares are trading at $5 a share, the company is said to have a "market cap" of $500 million. Some money managers prefer to invest in small stocks, and others prefer large-cap issues. While there is no official arbiter of what constitutes "small" and "large" stocks, _The Wall Street Journal_ currently sets the dividing point at a market cap of $1.5 billion. Any company with a market cap of less than that is considered a small stock, and any company with a larger market cap is considered a large company. Some money managers, recognizing that there is an awfully wide gulf between a "large" company with a market cap of $1.6 billion and a company like Microsoft, with a market cap of $390 billion, differentiate themselves as "midcap" investors, who generally confine themselves to stocks with a market cap of between $1.5 billion and $5 billion.

From the professional money managers' point of view there are advantages and disadvantages to each size category. Large-cap stocks tend to be well-established companies, although they can certainly be experiencing problems at any given time. More to the point, though, they will have a relatively large "float," or number of shares outstanding, and will thus usually be more "liquid," or easily traded, than a much smaller stock. For example, if you wanted to buy or sell one hundred thousand shares of General Motors at any given moment, there's a good chance the transaction could be done in a matter of minutes because GM is a highly liquid stock.

Large stocks have another advantage over small stocks. Bluntly put, it is power. One need look no further than the government's recent antitrust case against Microsoft to witness that power. The company brought enormous influence to bear on suppliers, customers, and even governments to get what it wanted. Even if a big company gets into trouble, the economic and political clout it wields will often get it benefits that can stave off or ameliorate the worst effects of whatever problems it is having. As I pointed out earlier in the chapter, value investors often prefer large companies because they're simply much more difficult to kill.

But large stocks also tend to get far more attention from Wall Street. Batteries of analysts are constantly poking and probing a company like General Electric, trying to determine how each of its many businesses is doing and to predict accurately what the company will earn each quarter. For anyone who believes in the efficient market hypothesis, that isn't good news. It leaves little room for the average investor to discover any inefficiencies that can be used to make an outsize profit.

Finally, large companies generally have a difficult time growing at above-average rates. Even the best-run big companies can't achieve average annual growth rates of more than about 20 percent for any sustained period of time, and the vast majority are far below that.

Small stocks tend to be very different. The typical small company is relatively young and not well established. But more important, it usually has a relatively small float. A professional money manager who decides to buy one hundred thousand shares of a small company will find not only that it takes hours or maybe days to accomplish the transaction, but also that in the course of buying or selling it becomes obvious to others in the market that something unusual is happening to the stock, causing them to try to take advantage of it. The result may be that when a money manager begins adding a small stock to a portfolio the price quickly rises from, say, $12 a share to $14 a share.

Small companies often have little power. Customers pressure them for price concessions and play them off against one another. Suppliers worry whether small companies will pay their bills on time, and small companies rarely have much, if any, clout with the government. Hundreds of small public companies fail every year, resulting in total losses for investors who owned the stock.

But there are advantages to being small, at least from a potential stockholder's point of view. Small companies can grow incredibly fast, at least in the first few years of their evolution toward becoming big companies. Since few analysts follow small companies, it appears that there probably is a better chance for an individual investor to discover unrealized value here than in the large-cap universe.

THE MYTH OF IPOS

You've doubtless read about the huge gains that new issues of stock in Internet companies post on their first days of trading. Wouldn't you like to be part of that game? Well, when I first began covering the financial markets more than a few years ago, I rapidly concluded that individual investors had no business dealing with initial public offerings (IPOs). It was obvious to me that the only IPOs that came the way of individuals were those that the big—and smart—institutional investors wouldn't touch. The good stuff was reserved by the big investment banking houses that underwrote the issues for their best clients: pension funds, mutual funds, and other large investors.

Times have changed. Increasingly brokerage firms are making shares of respectable IPOs available to individual investors. In other words, if you're a good individual client, your Merrill Lynch broker might get you one hundred shares of the same IPO that Fidelity is buying for some of its aggressive funds. But while times have changed, my opinion of IPOs hasn't. My conclusion is that most individuals should just stay away from IPOs. The reasons for that conclusion, however, are different. The fact remains that some schlocky IPOs still get palmed off on innocent and unwary individual investors. But as the IPO frenzy grows and more individuals clamor for shares, it makes sense for the investment bankers to let them in on the initial offerings, simply because in their emotional hysteria (often fueled by Internet chat rooms touting the IPO) these individuals bid the prices up to incredible levels, allowing the underwriters to make huge sums as they sell the shares they held in the fledgling company. And even when the IPO is a well-known company underwritten by a reputable investment bank, there remain two problems for individuals. First is the outright long-term performance of IPOs. A *Wall Street Journal* story on IPOs in 1998 summed it up this way: "When the history of the 1990s bull market is written, one of the more intriguing postscripts will be that it has given birth to so many new companies that created so little wealth." Consider the statistics: in the ten years from 1988 to 1998, of the 4,900 companies that became publicly traded, nearly 30 percent, as of 1998, were no longer listed on any market. Most had been delisted after failing to meet the minimum standards of their stock exchange. About 25 percent had been bought or merged into another company. And of the 70 percent or so still trading, a study done by U.S. Bancorp Piper Jaffray showed that the median annual return was a paltry 2.4 percent, less than what an investor could have earned in a simple and relatively safe money market account. In that same period stocks of well-established companies—the so-called blue-chip stocks—rose more than fourfold.

I still recall the frenzy that surrounded the IPO of an Internet start-up company called Theglobe.com. Underwriters at Bear Stearns brought the stock public at $9 a share. The first real trade occurred seconds later at an astounding $87 a share. Thousands of individual investors who had placed orders to buy "at the market" wound up with shares they would never have considered buying at such an extremely high price. And as it dawned on many of them that the stock was overpriced (and, more important, that they were facing a huge bill from their broker), widespread selling forced the price down to $32 in the subsequent week. Still, perhaps those frenzied investors learned a lesson from their experience, albeit an expensive one: Never, ever, enter an "at the market" order for an IPO. By setting a maximum price to be paid for the shares of a company coming public, an investor risks missing out on acquiring a piece of the new company. But thousands of investors fervently wished they had missed out on Theglobe.com's shares.

Such activity is, of course, unusual. More frequently the stock comes public at a certain price, rises modestly from that level, then settles down or even declines below its offering price. Over the long haul, the majority don't do much. Part of the problem is that when one company with a new idea or product goes public, competitors tend to follow it quickly to market. The result: too many companies trying to do the same thing. Only a few will survive, and even they won't be able to match investors' expectations. When their earnings eventually turn disappointing, analysts drop coverage, institutional investors lose interest, and both trading volumes and prices fall. I still remember the excitement that greeted the initial public offering of Boston Chicken, which went public at $10 a share and soared to $25.25 the first day. It eventually hit a high of $41.50 in 1996. In 1998 it filed for protection under Chapter 11 of the Bankruptcy Code, the victim of an over-ambitious expansion program. There are exceptions, of course, such as Dell and America Online. But picking winners like that out of the thousands of companies that go public is simply too difficult.

Even if it weren't so difficult to pick the winners, the brokerage industry is stacking the deck against the little guy through a practice called "flipping." When an investment bank allocates or grants shares of an IPO to a favored institutional client, that client is under no obligation to hold the shares. If the price soars in the opening minutes of trading for a particularly hot new offer, the institutional investors will "flip" the shares—that is, sell them after holding them for just a matter of minutes—and book a tidy profit. The individual investor who was allocated shares in the same IPO, however, is often warned by his or her broker that as a condition of receiving the shares they must be held for a specified period, such as ten days or thirty days. Should the individual choose to sell the shares before that period has expired, the broker likely won't let him or her have any future IPOs. The reason for this double standard is that a company that has just gone public doesn't like to see its shares sold just minutes after they were bought, even at a profit.

It's hoping that investors will want to own its shares for a long time. By issuing some shares to individuals with the caveat that they can't sell for a specified period of time, the investment banks underwriting the issue can guarantee some measure of stability for the stock. The investment banks can't put that same stricture on their institutional clients because they need the high initial demand that only such investors can provide to get the new stock launched. The situation for individual investors may change. After *The Wall Street Journal* exposed the practice of institutional flipping while individuals were implicitly forced to hold their shares of IPOs, the Securities and Exchange Commission opened an investigation into the practice, but as of this writing it has yet to take concrete action to stop it. In any event, the combination of poor performance of the majority of IPOs and the restrictions placed on individual investors by brokers leads me to conclude that most individuals shouldn't waste their time or money on IPOs. There's plenty of time to make money in the stocks of good companies after they've established a track record.

FOREIGN STOCKS

So far our stock discussion has centered on stocks of companies headquartered in the United States. But the U.S. stock markets represent less than 40 percent of the total stock market capitalization in the world. Why on earth would you want to ignore that other 60-plus percent?

Fear is usually the reason investors cite for not venturing abroad. And there's no question that the world outside our borders can be upsetting. Only a hermit living in a cave doesn't know that disaster struck many of the Asian economies in 1997, sending their stock markets into a devastating plunge, and that Russia's economy and markets imploded in 1998. If an individual investor needed confirmation that investing abroad is fraught with danger, those events would have done the trick. Yet at the same time that people were so focused on the disasters, most of Europe was moving steadily toward merging into a grand economic union that occurred officially on January 1, 1999. Not only will that union almost certainly bolster the European economy, but it will also help foster the creation and growth of new companies, many of which will be extremely profitable and eventually become world-class powers in their industries. And returning to Asia for a moment, do you really think that the smart, industrious people of Korea, Singapore, Hong Kong, or Taiwan are going to be held back for long by the economic upset of 1997? In 1999 stock markets in those countries turned in a stunningly positive performance. In retrospect, the crises in those markets were spectacular buying opportunities. I'm convinced there are great opportunities for investment outside the United States.

And it isn't just opportunities that draw me abroad. As you probably already know, diversification is the hallmark of a good investor, and foreign stocks add diversification in two important areas. First, they expose investors to other economies, which are likely to move in different cycles from those of the U.S. economy. Second, they expose U.S. investors to different currencies, which also move in different ways vis-à-vis the U.S. dollar. I won't argue that you should have 60 percent of your portfolio abroad, but I do suggest that you have up to 20 percent of it outside the United States as long as you are cognizant of and willing to take the risks. But investing in foreign stocks is easier said than done. To buy individual foreign stocks, you often must set up foreign brokerage accounts, which are both expensive and troublesome. Then you have to deal with the currency exchanges in different countries. And while it may be true that foreign markets are less efficient than U.S. markets and thus present the diligent investor with opportunities to find undiscovered gems, doing the necessary research is fearsomely expensive. There are some foreign stocks that are traded on U.S. stock exchanges in the form of something called "American Depositary Receipts" (ADRs). An ADR represents ownership of shares in a foreign company (the shares actually stay in the home country) and it is traded just like other stocks on the New York Stock Exchange and the NASDAQ market. ADRs are quoted in dollars (the price moves in an ADR reflect not only demand for the underlying shares, but also any changes in the currency relationships between the dollar and whatever the home currency is for the stock in question) every day in *The Wall Street Journal*, and the stocks are usually liquid enough that trades of a thousand shares or less can be executed quickly. Using ADRs, a U.S. investor can buy stocks in any of more than fifty countries, including, at last check, Zimbabwe. But it's still difficult to know as much about the underlying companies as the pros know (let alone more), so even if there are inefficiencies abroad, you're still at a disadvantage in trying to find them.

THE PARADOX

In the end, stocks confront investors with a real paradox. There's no question they are the best possible assets to own in a long-term investment program. Yet it appears that some form of the efficient market hypothesis makes it extremely difficult, if not impossible, to pick winning stocks with any consistent success. So what's a rational investor to do? The answer—If you can't beat 'em, join 'em—is laid out in chapter 4. But first let's pay a brief visit to bonds, the safety net in anyone's long-term portfolio.

3

BONDS:

The Safety Net

BONDS ARE SCHIZOPHRENIC INVESTMENTS. A U.S. Treasury bond is one of the safest investments anyone can make; the three-month Treasury note is regarded throughout the world as the benchmark for risk-free investing. Yet bonds can be immensely dangerous, too. It was bond trading that nearly sank Long-Term Credit Management, the vaunted hedge fund run by a fabled bond whiz and two Nobel Prize–winning economics laureates. Their huge bets on global bond moves went horribly wrong in the fall of 1998 and threatened to disrupt financial markets around the world until some of the fund's biggest creditors agreed to bail it out.

How you use bonds in a diversified, long-term investment portfolio will determine how risky they are for you. My view of bonds is pretty simple: They're for safety and certainty and nothing else. Long- and intermediate-term U.S. government bonds have a historical average annual return of just over 5 percent. With inflation running at an average annual rate of 3.1 percent, bonds clearly are far inferior to stocks as vehicles for building wealth. Of course, bonds can provide a steady stream of income. But because the income is taxed at ordinary income rates, it takes a whole lot of bonds to produce enough income to match the gains you would get over time from stocks. For example, a portfolio of stocks valued at $500,000 can be expected to produce an *average* annual return of 10 percent, or $50,000 before taxes. To get that same pretax return from Treasury bonds your portfolio would need to be worth nearly $1 million. And since your stock gains will be taxed at lower capital gains rates when you take them out, it would take well over $1 million in bonds to provide the same after-tax income. Granted, stock returns are very volatile. But if you built in a 50 percent margin of error for down years, you would still need only $750,000 in stocks to equal the returns from a $1 million portfolio of bonds. All this, of course, presumes that you are indeed a long-term investor and are making all your assumptions based on an investment horizon of ten years or more.

While you almost certainly won't build huge wealth by investing solely in bonds, don't reach the conclusion that they're a waste of time and effort. Used in the proper proportions, bonds can inject a note of stability into an overall portfolio, providing reassurance in times of stock market stress. And many people who are near or in retirement (which is to say past the age of substantial wealth accumulation) may want to rely more heavily on the certainty of income from bonds, even if that means a somewhat reduced standard of living.

However, although bonds can certainly be a useful part of an overall investment portfolio, they present a set of vexing problems to any long-term investor. The result of those problems is that it is difficult for many investors to decide how to approach bonds. Do you own individual bonds or mutual funds? What kinds of bonds? Treasurys, tax-free munis, or corporate bonds? Long-term bonds or short-term bonds? And where do you buy them? Most of this chapter will be devoted to unraveling some of the many complexities of bonds in an effort to steer you to the best solution for your needs. I'll make it very clear where my preference lies: inflation-indexed Treasury bonds, especially if you can park them in an IRA or other tax-advantaged account. But, as I'll explain, they aren't perfect. I just think they're better than anything else in the bond field if you truly want to use bonds as the control rods in a long-term portfolio devoted primarily to sometimes volatile stock investments.

How to Think About Bonds

There are two ways to use bonds in an investment portfolio: to obtain regular, predictable income (the approach I advocate) or to try to achieve capital gains (the approach Long-Term Capital Management took, with such disastrous consequences). We'll deal first with the most conservative way to use bonds. Not only does it produce safe, predictable income, it is also extremely easy to understand.

A bond is merely an agreement between a borrower and a lender stating the terms of a loan. A lender (the bondholder) agrees to advance a certain amount of money (the principal) to a borrower (the bond issuer). In exchange the borrower agrees to repay the loan in full at some future date (the maturity), as well as to pay a certain amount of interest periodically (the yield). Let's say the U.S. Treasury issued a ten-year bond in January 2001 with a yield of 5 percent. That means the owner of that bond (the lender) has lent the Treasury $1,000. The owner can expect the Treasury to repay that $1,000 at maturity in January 2011. Over the ten years the owner of the bond will receive $50 annually in two semiannual installments of $25 each.

The most obvious concern in considering a bond for investment is the "yield" it produces—that is, the interest that is paid to you for loaning your money. The yield on any bond *when it is issued* is determined by several factors. By far the most important determinant of yield is inflation or, more accurately, inflation expectations. Since most bonds are fixed-income securities (the rate of return and maturity date are stated—"fixed"—when the bond is issued), rising inflation can eat into the value of a bond's yield and principal. Consider that a 5 percent bond yields a "real return" of 3 percent if inflation is running at an annual rate of 2 percent (5 percent yield minus 2 percent inflation). That same bond yields zero if inflation is 5 percent, and it has a negative return—the bondholder actually loses money, or at least purchasing power—if inflation runs at 6 percent. Further, the longer the maturity of the bond, the greater the risk that inflation will occur and the greater the damage inflation can do. That explains why long-term bonds tend to have higher yields than short-term bonds issued by the same entity. Inflation expectations also explain why bonds issued at different times by the same agency with the same maturity— ten-year bonds issued by the Treasury, for instance—are issued with widely different yields. The bonds that are issued with high yields come out when investors are particularly worried about inflation; those that are issued at relatively low yields are sold when the inflation outlook seems tame.

A second large determinant of the yield on a bond stems from the creditworthiness of the issuer. Investors ask a simple question: How likely is it that the issuer will be willing and able to repay my principal when the bond matures? A bond issuer that cannot repay principal or that stops paying interest is said to have defaulted. Default risk explains the large difference in yields on bonds of the same maturity that are issued by different entities, ranging from the relatively low rates offered by the U.S. Treasury, which is assumed to have no risk of default (after all, it can either raise taxes or print money to repay bondholders), to the very high yields we see on bonds issued by ailing companies (often called "junk bonds") and governments of emerging markets (Russia effectively defaulted on its bonds in August 1998, much to the shock of even the savviest Wall Street bond traders).

That, in a nutshell, is how investing in bonds for safety works. But as you'll find with bonds, things are never quite as simple as they seem. The next section deals with the ways in which bond values can change and how individual investors (like you) often don't know—and, worse, can't learn—important details about bonds they may think about owning. You should understand this stuff for two reasons: It will probably help you narrow your choices of which bonds to use in your own portfolio, and it will explain why, if you wind up selling bonds through necessity or to capture some additional gains beyond the interest payments you expect to receive, you get the price you get. Certainly, if you intend to trade bonds with an eye toward maximizing your gains, you need to know how the process works. In this next section you'll get a briefing (I promise it truly will be brief) on such arcane topics as liquidity, yield to maturity, call provisions, and lots of other complicated-sounding stuff. Then you'll know just enough to be dangerous (to yourself). If you still want to play that game, you'll need to get your hands on a good finance text and really learn the amazing complexities of the bond market.

BOND YIELDS AND BOND PRICES

Let's start with the single thing that tends to most confuse novice bond investors: yields and prices. Simply stated, as the price of a bond rises, the yield falls. Conversely, if the price falls, the yield rises. That relationship occurs because the value of a bond lies in the size of its income stream. Here's a simplified explanation of how it works. Let's say a company wants to raise money by issuing a ten-year bond. The accumulated inflation expectations and other wisdom of all the people who want to buy that bond results in a coupon of 8 percent, and the bond sells at par (you give the issuer $1,000 for a bond with a $1,000 face amount). In exchange you can expect to receive $80 each year and to receive your $1,000 back at the end of ten years.

Now we'll complicate the picture by assuming that inflation rises more than expected soon after the bond is issued. You're now kicking yourself for buying the bond and want to get rid of it. But other investors are worried about inflation and won't be satisfied with an 8 percent income stream. They want a higher return. The solution: The bond will sell at less than par so that the yield will rise. You might find someone, for example, who is willing to accept a return of 8.33 percent. To get that, he will pay you just $960 for your $1,000 bond. The calculation is relatively simple: Once he owns your bond he will get the same $80 per year that you were receiving. But if he paid less than $1,000 for the bond, that $80 annual payment will represent a higher percentage yield. In this case, divide the $80 annual payout by the $960 purchase price and see the answer: 8.33 percent.

Consider the opposite situation: Inflation unexpectedly drops soon after you buy the bond. Now other investors are kicking themselves for not buying that bond and want to own it. But you'll sell it only if someone pays you a premium for it. We'll say someone comes along and offers you $1,050 for your $1,000 bond. She, too, will continue to collect the $80 annual payments once she owns the bond. But because she paid more than $1,000 for it, the yield will be lower than 8 percent. In this case, dividing the $80 annual payout by a purchase price of $1,050 produces a yield of 7.62 percent.

This simple example illustrates how an investor can make or lose money by trading a bond. If you were the investor in the example above who bought the bond before inflation unexpectedly rose, you took a loss on the sale of your bond. If you were the second investor, you realized a gain when you sold. But it is important to understand that if you bought that same bond when it was issued and held it for ten years until it matured, none of those price and yield changes would have affected you. You would have received your $80 annual payments (which would, of course, have been more or less valuable depending upon what inflation was doing), and you would have received your $1,000 back at the end of ten years. The goal of bond *trading*—as opposed to bond *investing*—is to earn a total return (yield plus price moves) that is better than yield alone. If events are favorable, the gains from trading bonds can be impressive. But if the tables are turned, the losses can be disturbing. And the trouble is, no one—not even the smartest and highest-paid bond traders on Wall Street—can consistently predict what will make bond prices rise or fall.

BOND PRICING: WHAT YOU DON'T KNOW CAN HURT YOU

If uncertainty about the direction of bond prices isn't enough to discourage you from pursuing bond trading, I'll add yet another hurdle: When you buy or sell most bonds, you don't know if you're getting a fair price. In fact, you often don't even *know* the price. The bond market is archaic and rife with abuses that are particularly difficult for an individual investor to even know, much less overcome.

Let's compare bond pricing to stock pricing. Recall from our earlier explanations that on the New York Stock Exchange (NYSE) the price of a stock lies somewhere between the bid price and the ask price quoted by the specialists on the stock exchange floor who handle individual issues. The "spread," or difference, between the bid and ask prices is often one-sixteenth of a dollar, or 6¼ cents. Each time a trade occurs, the price at which it took place is recorded and made public within seconds. As a result, everyone, from the head of the trading desk at Merrill Lynch to the individual investor with one hundred shares of General Electric to sell, knows within a very tight range what they can get for their shares at a given moment. Stocks that trade on the National Association of Securities Dealers market are handled a little differently. Dealers who make a market in any given issue constantly post on an electronic network their bid and ask prices. Those, too, are frequently as small as one sixteenth of a dollar, although less liquid issues may have spreads of one eighth or even one fourth of a dollar. Just like the NYSE, NASDAQ posts its price transactions virtually instantly for anyone to see.

But bonds, with the exception of a few hundred issues traded on exchanges, don't work like that at all. The bond market is, for the most part, designed for and run by professional investors. Most bonds are traded "over the counter" by a network of dealers. Big investors wielding millions of dollars have the financial clout to demand the best prices from dealers and to discover, through comparative quotes, the prevailing prices of bonds. Individuals, who typically buy or sell less than $100,000 of bonds at one time, are in no such position of power. Nowhere will an individual investor find prices of bonds posted, and the prices at which transactions occur aren't made public. Indeed, with millions of separate bond issues available, some don't trade for days, weeks, or even months. The result: an almost total lack of bond price transparency. An individual investor seldom knows the real price of a bond at the time of purchase, how that price changes from day to day while the bond is held, or even the real price at the time of sale. Typically a dealer will charge an individual investor an undisclosed premium, called a "markup," when a bond is purchased, and another undisclosed premium, called a "markdown," when the bond is sold. Those undisclosed fees can take 7 percent or more out of any potential profit on a bond purchase and sale. If stocks were quoted in the same way as bonds are bought and sold, the spread between the price to buy and sell would be measured in whole dollars instead of less than seven cents.

What's more, there is little uniformity to bond pricing. A study done in 1998 for *The Wall Street Journal* found a difference of almost 2.5 percent, or $2,500, in the prices offered by ten brokerage firms for two blocks of municipal bonds with a face value of $50,000 each. Even if you're willing to spend the time to try to garner quotes from ten different bond brokers, chances are they won't even give you a quote unless you actually open an account.

Bond dealers argue that unlike stockbrokers, who serve mostly as middlemen in a transaction, bond dealers actually own the bonds in question and thus take on the risk that the market will move against them, reducing the value of the bonds in their inventory. They also point out that while some fifteen thousand public stocks are traded in the United States, there are literally millions of bonds, many of which trade very seldom, thus making it difficult to calculate the real demand and set a price.

I don't see any point in getting involved in a lengthy debate with the bond dealer community about what kind of compensation they're entitled to for taking the risk of holding bonds in inventory. My point is very simple: The markups that bond dealers charge present an almost insurmountable barrier to making any real profits in bond trading and sap a large portion of the yield that even a buy-and-hold investor can hope to receive. That's why I'm such a big advocate of a program the U.S. Treasury runs called "Treasury Direct" (details to follow). By purchasing government bonds directly from the Treasury at an auction, even the smallest individual investor can avoid the confusion and expense of buying from a dealer. But even there, if you must sell your Treasury bond before maturity, you'll encounter the problem of a markdown.

CALCULATING BOND RETURNS

Figuring the return an investor derives from a bond ranges from immensely simple to enormously complicated. It all depends on how the bond is used. The simplest calculation involves a bond purchased at par and held to maturity. It will yield its coupon: a ten-year 5 percent Treasury bond will yield 5 percent. The next simplest calculation involves a bond purchased sometime after issue at a premium or discount. An investor can calculate the current yield simply by dividing the coupon payment by the purchase price, as we did in our examples illustrating the inverse relationship of price and yield. This calculation is done for you on the relatively few bonds whose prices are quoted daily in *The Wall Street Journal*.

But the current yield doesn't take into account the principal amount a bondholder will receive at maturity. Instead a more complex formula produces the "yield to maturity" (YTM), a figure that takes into account both the coupon payment and the gains or losses experienced by purchasing a bond at a premium or discount to its face value. Fortunately most business calculators contain programs to do the calculations of yield to maturity. Do-it-yourselfers can find the formula in most finance textbooks, and a bond dealer will be glad to do it for you (just remember he controls the price at which you will purchase a bond). Yet even the calculator produces an inaccurate figure because it assumes that the coupon payments are reinvested at the same interest rate as the bond yield. But because interest rates are changing constantly, it is virtually certain that coupon payments will be invested at higher or lower rates over the life of a bond. If the coupons are invested, on average, at a higher rate, the yield to maturity will be higher than calculated. Coupon payments invested at a lower rate will produce a lower yield to maturity than calculated. And coupon payments that are spent rather than invested will result in a markedly lower yield to maturity.

As if it weren't already complicated enough, there's another wrinkle affecting bond prices and yield calculations: call provisions. Most corporate bonds and some government issues contain a clause that allows the issuer to "call" the bond—that is, pay it off early. A bond typically is called if the issuer finds that interest rates have fallen substantially below the levels at which the bond was originally issued. The issuer can lower its overall financing cost by selling a new bond at a lower coupon reflecting the improved interest rate picture and using part of the proceeds of that sale to redeem its earlier bonds from holders. If, for instance, a company issued a ten-year 8 percent coupon bond five years ago and now finds that interest rates have fallen substantially, it may issue a new ten-year bond at 6 percent. An investor holding a $10,000 8 percent bond will receive a notice that the bond has been called and will be repaid the $10,000 principal five years early. Not only will the investor no longer continue to collect $800 a year, he or she will have to reinvest the $10,000 at the new lower interest rates that now prevail. Thus it can be useful to calculate a bond's yield to call, using the same formula for calculating the yield to maturity but substituting the first date at which the bond can be called for the maturity date.

Had enough bond market mechanics? Bear with me for just one more paragraph. Remember how earlier in the chapter I pointed out that for the most part longer-maturity bonds carry higher yields to compensate for the increased risk that inflation might rise over time? Well, if you're going to be a bond trader, you need to also know that maturity affects price volatility. Simply put, the longer the maturity of a bond, the more its price and yield will move in response to the same event. A ten-year 10 percent coupon bond priced at $1,000 at issue will drop to a price of $885 if investors demand a yield of 12 percent. But a thirty-year 10 percent bond will plunge to $838 if investors demand a yield of 12 percent. On the other hand, the price of the ten-year bond will rise to $1,136 if conditions allow the yield to fall to 8 percent; that of the thirty-year bond will soar to $1,226 under the same conditions. The lesson to be drawn is that gamblers who want to make the most on a bond trade—and can stomach the possibility of big losses—should buy the longest-maturity bonds, while investors who fear they may have to sell a bond early for some reason should stick to shorter-maturity issues.

There's more that the avid student of bonds can delve into, including such concepts as duration and convexity, but I think I've made my point about bonds: It's easy to use them as a safety net, but very difficult to use them well as a trading tool. Even when you use them well to trade, the returns are likely to be lower than what you can realize from stocks. So let's return to the safety theme and examine various kinds of bonds and the benefits and dangers they pose to individual investors who want to use them conservatively. Before going to the menu, we want to explain two relatively simple concepts that will help you evaluate bonds for possible purchase.

THE BOND MENAGERIE

There are lots of different kinds of bonds. They vary mostly in terms of maturity (from thirty days to fifty years), the creditworthiness of their issuers, and their liquidity. What follows is a summary of the kinds of bonds you might want to use in your portfolio, with the pros and cons noted. I think it will be obvious which bonds I prefer, but in the end the need for a higher return may be more important to you than inflation protection or the costs of transactions. That's a decision you'll have to make.

TREASURY BILLS, NOTES, AND BONDS

As I explained earlier, Treasury bonds are the safest fixed-income investment you can make. But there are different kinds of Treasury bonds and different maturities, so simply to say you want to invest in Treasury bonds isn't enough. The two most striking features of virtually every type of Treasury bond are safety and convenience. By safety, of course, I'm referring to the risk of default. It simply doesn't exist for Treasury bonds. The government will not default (if it does, you and I will have a lot more to worry about than being repaid the money we lent the government). And by convenience I mean that purchasing Treasury bonds is about as easy—and cheap—as it gets. Using the aforementioned Treasury Direct program, you and any other small investor can purchase Treasury bonds directly from the government, right alongside such giant players as Goldman Sachs and Morgan Stanley, free of any fees or commissions.

The Treasury also offers a very large range of maturities from which you can choose. You can buy anything from a three-month bill to a thirty-year bond, although you had better hurry if you want to load up on thirty-year issues (not a good idea!); the Treasury is phasing out issuance of these long-term bonds to save money. That will leave the ten-year issue as the "benchmark" against which virtually all other bonds, both foreign and domestic, government and corporate, are measured. The short end of the Treasury's menu of notes and bonds, ranging from three months to one year, can be extremely safe and low-cost places to park a wad of cash that you know you'll need at a certain date in the future. Just be aware that short-term notes are priced differently from longer-term bonds. Recall that when you purchase a long-term Treasury bond you pay $1,000, then receive periodic interest payments until the bond matures, at which time you get your principal back. Short-term bills, however, are sold at a discount, which simply means that you pay less than the face amount. When the note or bill matures you receive the face amount. The difference between what you pay and what you receive at maturity is the yield you earn.

For all their desirable features, however, there's one thing that plain vanilla Treasury bonds can't protect you from: inflation. Of course, when the bonds are issued at auction (where you buy them if you participate in Treasury Direct), the price they bring reflects the best judgment of all the purchasers, you as well as Goldman Sachs, about the likely impact of inflation. Keep in mind, however, that Goldman, which probably is buying a few more bonds at auction than you are, doesn't plan to hang on to them very long. Instead it will resell them to other investors or trade them to try to make a profit on interest rate moves. So Goldman's assessment of the likely course of inflation is based on a completely different set of circumstances from your own. If you buy a ten-year note that yields 6 percent, you are probably hoping that inflation during that ten-year period will average less than 4 percent, giving you a "real return" (not including taxes, of course) of more than 2 percent. But if inflation gets out of hand during the decade you hold the bond, it could substantially reduce or even wipe out your "real returns." You could even wind up losing money (or at least purchasing power) on what is widely considered the safest investment in the world.

That's why I'm a big fan of a recent Treasury innovation: inflation-indexed bonds. With these new bonds, which can also be bought at auction through Treasury Direct, you not only get the safety inherent in any U.S government bond, you also get protection from inflation. Other than inflation-indexed savings bonds, which we'll discuss shortly, this is the only way I know that you can invest in a fixed-income product that inflation can't hurt. The interest rate that an inflation-indexed Treasury bond pays is set at the auction through the process of supply and demand. Recent auctions have produced bonds that yield about 4 percent. I know what you're going to say: "Four percent? I can get 6 percent on the regular Treasury bond!" That's true. But the regular Treasury bond has to pay you what amounts to a premium to try to protect you from future inflation. That premium may be sufficient to do that, but it also may fall short, as we discussed earlier. Since the inflation-indexed bond is guaranteed to protect you from inflation, it doesn't need to pay that same premium. With inflation running at a little more than 2 percent, you essentially locked in a permanent life-of-issue real return of about 2 percent (close to the historical average return) if you bought that recent inflation-indexed bond.

Once the bond is issued, the Treasury monitors inflation as measured by a particular form of the Consumer Price Index. If inflation continues to rise after the bond is issued, the principal amount of your bond (they're issued in amounts of as little as $1,000) is periodically adjusted upward by the amount of inflation. In other words, if inflation rose 2 percent in the year after you bought a $1,000 inflation-indexed bond, your principal would in-

crease by 2 percent, to $1,020. Not only that, but your periodic in-
terest payments would remain 4 percent on the increased amount
of principal, so that your income, too, would keep pace with inflation. No matter how bad inflation gets, the bond earns the same
real return and the purchasing power of the $1,000 investment re-
mains steady over the life of the bond. What happens if instead of
inflation, the nation goes through a period of deflation, in which
overall prices fall? The value of your bond will be adjusted downward, although never below the $1,000 par value. The result is
that you will never know in advance exactly what your income or
principal will be over the life of the bond. But you do know that
the underlying value of the bond and the value of its income
stream will not be eroded by inflation.

So why aren't these the perfect investment for people seeking
assured income? There's one little glitch that theoretically could
become a very big glitch: taxes. Recall that we used in our example of how inflation-indexed bonds work a $1,000 bond one year
after it was issued in an environment of 2 percent inflation. The
value of the bond was adjusted upward by $20 to keep pace with
inflation. Well, Uncle Sam giveth, and he taketh away. He consid-
ers that $20 increase in the bond's value to be income, and he
wants his cut of it. So if you're in the 28 percent tax bracket, you'll
owe the IRS $5.60 in additional income tax for that year. In effect
you're giving up a portion of your inflation protection in the form
of taxes. Under some scenarios in which inflation spikes sharply
higher, taxpayers in the highest brackets could actually wind up
owing more in taxes on the phantom income from their TIPs
(Treasury Inflation Protected bonds) than they receive in interest
payments, which would be disconcerting to say the least. The solution, if your circumstances allow it, is to load up your IRA or
other tax-advantaged account with TIPs while holding stocks
in nonadvantaged accounts. The question, of course, is whether
that tax burden is enough of a disincentive to avoid these bonds.
The answer depends on several factors—your tax rate, the price
of the bonds compared with regular Treasury issues, and how
worried you are about inflation. With inflation quiescent these
past few years, there hasn't been much demand from individual investors for these bonds, so the prices have been extraordinarily cheap and presented investors with a great buying
opportunity. But the next time we see a surge of prices—and I'm

certain it will happen, although I have no idea when—inflation-indexed bonds will begin to look very, very attractive.

No matter whether you buy plain vanilla or inflation-indexed bonds, if you anticipate that you might have to sell a Treasury note or bond before maturity, remember that the longer the maturity, the more volatile the price. If interest rates have fallen since you purchased your Treasury security, a thirty-year bond will have risen more in price than a ten-year Treasury. Conversely, if rates rise, your thirty-year bond will have lost considerably more of its value than a ten-year Treasury if you need to sell. You can, of course, buy Treasurys of virtually any maturity simply by asking a broker to get you an existing bond that matures on whatever target date you wish. You will pay for that privilege, however, not only because a broker will charge you a premium, but also because such bonds (called "off-the-run" bonds) don't trade nearly as frequently as the latest auctioned issue (called "on-the-run" bonds).

TREASURY STRIPS OR ZERO-COUPON BONDS

Zero-coupon bonds can be had in any of several stripes: Treasury, municipal, or corporate. Given my decided bias toward Treasury bonds, I'll discuss so-called stripped Treasury bonds here; the dangers apply even more to other types of strips.

Zero-coupon bonds were created in the early 1980s, when clever investment bankers figured out they could separate the coupon payments of a bond from the principal (the coupons were "stripped" from the bonds, hence the name) and then sell the two pieces separately. Someone could choose to collect the income stream but not the principal, and someone else could elect to receive the principal but no periodic interest payments. For individual investors the attraction of zero-coupon bonds is that the principal part of the bond can be purchased at a steep discount since it doesn't offer any income (it has a "zero coupon"). The longer the maturity of the bond (in effect, the more income forgone), the greater the discount. A thirty-year bond that promises to pay $1,000 face amount can be purchased for between $200 and $300. Several aspects of zero coupons have made them immensely popular: the low purchase price, the freedom from worrying about reinvesting periodic interest payments, and the certainty of receiving a much larger sum on a certain date in the future. New parents love zero-coupons as planning tools for funding college educations more than a decade away.

But zero-coupon bonds, whether issued by the Treasury, a city, or a company, have some disadvantages that should cause most investors to think twice about how they're used. Even if you intend simply to hold the bond to maturity, you will face a vexing problem: Although zero-coupon bonds don't pay any semiannual interest, they are taxed as if they do. The Internal Revenue Service each year will want to collect taxes on what is called the "accreted interest" (the amount of interest you would have earned had your zero been a conventional bond). Taxes are irksome enough without having to pay taxes on money you didn't receive. This problem can be solved by holding zero-coupon bonds in individual retirement accounts or 401(k) accounts, where current income is not taxed.

The other problem with zero-coupons is price volatility. Because there is no steady income to cushion the effects of price changes, zero-coupon bond prices can move wildly. If rates rise, the prices of existing stripped bonds plunge. Of course, if rates fall, the prices soar. If you really want to try to make money trading bonds, zeroes are the weapon of choice, as long as you remember they can blow up in your face. Once you move beyond stripped Treasurys, which have essentially no default risk, you encounter all the same problems—big markups by dealers, lack of liquidity, and possible default risk—that are common to conventional municipal and corporate bonds. And as with every other kind of bond except inflation-indexed Treasurys, inflation could rise enough to cut severely into the purchasing power of your principal when it is returned to you.

U.S. GOVERNMENT SAVINGS BONDS

We're still on the subject of government bonds, so we'll take a quick diversion into savings bonds. With one exception, they don't have much to offer the serious investor. But because they are utterly simple, they make a nice gift to celebrate a new addition to the family or for a high school graduate. The problem is that they tend to offer rates lower than can be obtained from other sources, and they don't provide a steady stream of income.

Series EE savings bonds, like other direct government issues, have virtually no default risk. They have a twelve-year maturity, they are purchased from the government with no fees or commissions, and, like short-term notes, they are purchased at a discount (at exactly half the face value). Like zero-coupon bonds, savings bonds accrete interest; but unlike zeroes, you don't pay taxes on the accreted interest. The interest rate on savings bonds is calculated based on the yields of five-year Treasury notes and currently amounts to 90 percent of that amount, with interest accruing (but not paid) monthly. There is no secondary market for savings bonds (so you can neither gain nor lose if interest rates change), but the Treasury will allow you to redeem bonds early (a three-month interest penalty will be incurred if you redeem in the first five years of ownership).

If you hold a Series EE bond to maturity, it can be exchanged for a Series HH bond, delaying any taxes due on the maturing EE bond. HH bonds have a twenty-year maturity and actually pay interest to you every six months (sorry, the interest is taxable at the federal level, although not at the state and local level). HH bonds can be sold back to a bank or the Federal Reserve after six months of ownership.

The one savings bond that could have some appeal to investors is the I bond, an inflation-indexed savings bond that is very similar to its inflation-indexed Treasury cousins. I bonds are very similar to EE bonds, but rather than being purchased at half face value, they are bought for full face value. And unlike EE bonds, I bonds have two components. One component provides a fixed rate of return, determined by the Treasury, for the life of the bond. The other component is an inflation adjustment that is made every six months, either up or down depending on what inflation has done in the last six months. And while I bonds offer essentially the same kind of inflation protection offered by inflation-indexed Treasury bonds, they do so without the phantom tax burden that investors encounter if they hold inflation-indexed Treasury bonds outside a tax-advantaged account. So what's the problem with I bonds? Well, they don't provide any periodic income, and you're limited to purchases of $30,000 a year. That's a pretty low limit for someone with a substantial portfolio who is shifting from an aggressive stock strategy to a more conservative stock/bond combination in preparation for retirement.

GOVERNMENT AGENCY BONDS

There is a subset of what you can think of as government-like bonds that share some of the attributes of both government and corporate bonds. The issuers aren't really part of the federal government, but the government has chosen for its purposes to back them to the extent that default risk is slim or virtually nonexistent. Most of the bonds are issued by agencies that deal with housing: the Government National Mortgage Association (GNMA), the Federal National Mortgage Association (FNMA), and the Federal Home Loan Mortgage Corporation (FHLMC). You might not recognize those names, but you've probably heard references to their nicknames: Ginnie Mae, Fannie Mae, and Freddie Mac.

These agencies issue two kinds of bonds, but individual investors tend to be interested primarily in the more arcane of the two. The standard bonds are very like corporate issues with the extra measure of security afforded by the government's commitment to back these agencies.

The second type are called "pass-through, mortgage-backed bonds," and they have some peculiar and potentially useful features. The bonds start life as residential mortgages (loans made by financial institutions to individual purchasers of residential real estate). Thousands of these mortgages are purchased by Ginnie Mae, Fannie Mae, and Freddie Mac and assembled into mortgage pools. Parts of the pools are then sold to individual investors as bonds. But unlike other government bonds, mortgage-backed bonds pay interest on a monthly rather than a semiannual schedule. If you're particularly poor at managing your spending, it can be helpful to have a check arrive each month rather than every six months.

Another peculiarity is that each month's payment consists not only of the interest that homeowners pay on their mortgage loans (which is "passed through" to you, hence the name), but also a piece of the principal. If you have ever owned a home, you know that early in the life of a thirty-year mortgage most of the payments go to satisfy interest payments and only a tiny fraction is applied to reducing the principal amount of the loan. But as you continue to make your mortgage payments over the years, the amount of each month's payment devoted to satisfying interest declines, while the amount that pays down the principal rises. This affords individual investors a chance to manage their taxes by purchasing either relatively new mortgage-backed bonds, in which most of the monthly payments consist of taxable interest payments, or older, "seasoned" issues in which large chunks of the monthly payment are devoted to the nontaxable reduction of the principal. Since mortgage-backed bonds generally have higher yields than Treasury bonds, a high-income taxpayer can gain enough in untaxed monthly interest payments to make mortgage-backed bonds worthy of consideration.

But before you trash Treasurys to gain that extra bit of income, consider the downside of mortgage-backed bonds. You'll recall that these bonds are made up of thousands of mortgages. While most mortgages are written for thirty years, relatively few mortgages are carried through to maturity. Instead, homeowners find any number of reasons to sell the old homestead and buy a new one. As a result, the average mortgage lasts for only about seven years. Each time one of the homeowners in the pool of mortgages represented by your bond pays off a mortgage early, you get your cut of that principal repayment in your monthly check, which as a consequence varies in size from one month to the next. Eventually the vast majority of the mortgages are paid off early and you get your principal back. Early payoffs are more likely when interest rates are falling and homeowners are refinancing existing mortgages. The consequence for bondholders is that they may receive their principal much earlier than expected and face the prospect of reinvesting it at considerably lower rates than they had anticipated. That early redemption and consequent reinvestment risk, coupled with the brokerage fee required to purchase most mortgage-backed bonds, leaves me questioning the usefulness of these issues when compared with the certainty of a straightforward or inflation-indexed Treasury bond.

TAX-FREE MUNICIPAL BONDS

Believe me, every April I completely understand and sympathize with what must be one of the strongest driving forces in nature after food, sex, and sleep: the urge to avoid paying taxes. That urge has made tax-free municipal bonds one of the most popular of investment options for millions of taxpayers. Unfortunately, many of those investors don't fully understand the costs or the benefits of tax-free munis and may be sacrificing income or taking more risk than they wish.

The allure of muni bonds, of course, is that the income they pay is free of federal income taxes and, if issued by authorities in the state in which you live, free of state and local taxes, too. But that tax-free status means that the value of a municipal bond isn't the same for every investor, because investors have different tax situations. The higher your marginal tax rate, the more valuable a given muni bond will be to you. The table "Taxable Equivalent Yields" shows the yield that you have to obtain on a taxable bond to equal the tax-free yield from a muni bond at the stated yields. And the chart doesn't take into account the additional taxable yield you would need if you live in states like New York or New Jersey with their punishingly high income tax rates. Judging by the chart, an investor in the 15 percent bracket confronted with a choice between a muni bond yielding 4 percent tax-free and a Treasury bond yielding 5 percent would favor the taxable Treasury bond. But an investor in the 39.6 percent bracket would have to find a taxable bond paying 6.62 percent to get the same after-tax yield he or she would get from a 4 percent muni.

TAXABLE EQUIVALENT YIELDS

The amount investors in different tax brackets would have to earn on a taxable bond to equal the yield of a tax-free bond. State and local taxes would increase the amount an investor would have to earn from the taxable bond to equal the tax-free yield.

	Federal Tax Bracket			
Tax-Exempt Yield	15%	28%	31%	39.6%
4%	4.71%	5.56%	5.80%	6.62%
5%	5.88%	6.94%	7.25%	8.28%
6%	7.06%	8.33%	8.70%	9.93%
7%	8.24%	9.72%	10.14%	11.59%
8%	9.41%	11.11%	11.59%	13.25%
9%	10.59%	12.50%	13.04%	14.90%

Of course, the issuers of muni bonds know that their tax advantage gives them a leg up on most other kinds of fixed investments, so the bonds are priced to yield substantially less than taxable bonds. At the same time, muni bonds face the same risks as do most other non-Treasury bonds: default is possible; the credit-worthiness of the issuing party can rise or fall, affecting the price you would get if you had to sell a muni bond before it matured; there is often a call risk; and liquidity in the market is frequently poor, leaving you at the mercy of a broker and his or her fees when you buy or sell a muni bond. All of those risks, along with the possibility of higher than anticipated inflation during the life of the bond, dictate that muni bonds be substituted for Treasury bonds only when the taxable equivalent yield is substantial. Even then buyers should stick to issues rated A or better by Moody's *and* Standard & Poor's (if the two agencies' ratings differ markedly, investigate why; better yet, find another bond), and they should own lots of different issues for the safety that diversification provides. And before you put too much faith in ratings agencies, recall that both S&P and Moody's gave Orange County, California, debt high ratings before the county's $20 billion investment pool filed for bankruptcy late in 1994.

There are two types of municipal bonds. "General obligation municipal bonds" are the municipal equivalent of Treasury bonds: they're guaranteed by the taxing authority of the issuer. If the Treasury were in danger of defaulting on its bonds, it would raise taxes (or print more money). If a city or state is in danger of default, it, too, pledges to raise taxes (it can't print money, thank God) to meet its obligation.

A "revenue bond," on the other hand, is more akin to a corporate bond. The interest payments on a revenue bond are derived from the user fees collected by the issuer, be it a hospital, sewer system, or toll highway. If the issuer can't collect enough revenue to pay its obligations, there is no recourse but default. One way to try to head off such problems is to buy only muni bonds that are highly rated by the two major bond ratings services. Better yet, buy an insured muni bond. These securities are issued by municipalities that pay a premium to a bond insurance firm. Such bonds are almost always rated AAA. They'll have a lower yield than lower-rated bonds, but the peace of mind will be worth it. In any case, never, ever buy an unrated bond, no matter how attractive its yield may be.

A variant on revenue bonds is the "industrial revenue bond," which is used to promote industrial growth. Usually the bond is the obligation of and will be repaid by the corporation whose fa-

cilities it financed; thus the creditworthiness of the corporate issuer must be investigated before purchase. Most industrial revenue bonds today are issued as part of an effort to improve the
infrastructure of a community, such as building a waste treatment
or recycling center, an airport, or a harbor.

CORPORATE BONDS

Corporate bonds come in two varieties: investment-grade and
junk. The names say it all. Investment-grade bonds are for those of
you who, ignoring all my earlier advice about the difficulty of getting fair pricing from bond dealers, decide to go for the extra yield
available from corporate bonds. Keep in mind, however, that the
company that issued the bonds can neither print money nor tax its
clients to fulfill its obligations to bondholders. Instead the company can pay the interest due on its bonds only from its cash flow
and retained earnings. A recession could certainly jeopardize that
ability entirely or, less cataclysmic, could prompt the ratings agencies to downgrade an issuer (which means the company's outstanding bonds will fall in price). Again, for peace of mind stick
only with highly rated corporate issuers and quite a few of them to
get the safety of diversity. Then be prepared to get hit with
markups when you buy and markdowns when you sell. It's the
price of doing business with bond dealers.

"Junk" is the name that Wall Street (much to its regret) attached years ago to corporate bonds that are essentially an invita-
tion to gamble (the ratings label on these bonds calls them
"speculative," and Wall Street now prefers the moniker "high-
yield"). The bet can be very tempting. Junk bonds offer very attractive yields (when compared with everything else). But there's a
reason: The companies that issue them are on the slippery side of
the finance slope and may just plunge over the precipice.

Junk bonds can be created in one of two ways. The first is for
an investment-grade bond to be downgraded to the speculative
level because the issuer gets into some kind of trouble and its ability to pay interest and principal on its outstanding debt becomes
questionable. The second way is for a relatively small company
that needs to finance its expansion to rely on the credit markets instead of issuing stock in a public offering. In the mid-1990s the ex-

panding telecommunications industry, particularly wireless companies, needed to raise lots of money to build an expensive network of relay towers and switches. Because these companies couldn't reach the critical mass necessary to make profits without first building most of their networks, the equity market was closed to many of them, and they chose instead to issue bonds.

For the most part I'm opposed to investing in junk bonds. For one thing, a junk bond portfolio demands tremendous diversification to offset the risks; few individual investors can afford to buy an adequate number of different issues to achieve that level of diversification. But the real point is that an investor is taking too big a risk with money that is supposed to be invested safely. Take your risks in stocks, where the upside is virtually unlimited, and put your safe money in Treasurys.

BUILDING A BOND LADDER

Once you figure out which kinds of bonds you want to have in your portfolio, you've got to figure out when to buy them. The temptation, of course, is to load up on bonds when interest rates seem high and thus will afford you a good income. That would be a fine approach if bonds didn't have maturity dates. But unlike stocks, which can be held in perpetuity (or at least until the company goes broke or gets bought), bonds have a definite life span, and that's a problem. Let's say you load up with ten-year Treasury bonds when rates seem high. The trouble is, they may just *seem* high at the moment but may actually be headed a lot higher in the next five years or so, in which case you've missed the boat on really high rates. But more important, you've tied up a huge sum of money for ten years. You can get it back by selling the bonds before they mature, but that may force you to take a capital loss, and it will certainly cost you some part of your overall return to sell them through a bond dealer. And if you hold the bonds to maturity, you're suddenly confronted with a huge wad of cash that must be reinvested. If interest rates are unusually low at that point, you're stuck. The income you enjoyed from the high rates during the past ten years is going to drop substantially when you reinvest at the much lower rates that might prevail.

But don't worry, there's a solution to this vexing problem. It's called a "bond ladder," and it's an amazingly simple approach to building a portfolio of bonds. The only catch is that you have to think ahead. Way ahead. A bond ladder is constructed by periodically buying bonds of the same maturity. For example, if you're planning your bond portfolio far enough ahead—ten years is what I have in mind—you would buy perhaps $10,000 of ten-year inflation-indexed Treasury bonds at a Treasury auction. That becomes the first rung of your bond ladder. A year later you would buy another $10,000 of the new ten-year inflation-indexed Treasury bond at a Treasury auction. Now you have two rungs on your ladder, and you doubtless see where we're going with this: After ten years you'll have a ten-rung Treasury bond ladder, and your first rung will be maturing and can be reinvested in yet another batch of ten-year Treasurys.

The beauty of this approach is twofold. First, you're not timing the interest rate cycle and taking the risk of being trapped with your entire fixed-income portfolio left in the dust by rising interest rates. Instead, your periodic purchases smooth out your own returns regardless of what's happening to rates at any moment. Second, once the bond ladder is built, you will always be a relatively short time away from having access to a big chunk of your money if you need it (as the oldest rung in your ladder matures). If you don't need it, reinvest it and the ladder will stay intact. You can choose to build your ladder with smaller, more frequent rungs, the interval between being governed by how often you can buy the bonds of your choice. Auctions of various Treasury issues, for example, take place at different intervals, ranging from weekly to every six months. Of course, you can always visit a bond dealer and set up an instant ladder of whatever kinds of bonds you want drawn from the extensive inventory of already issued bonds in the marketplace, but that's a costly way to go about the process. Further, each rung needn't be the same size. Indeed, many people building a bond ladder in anticipation of retirement might want to increase the size of each new rung in order to slowly tilt their overall investment portfolio toward a more conservative stock/bond allocation.

A Word on Treasury Direct

Treasury bonds are among the most liquid securities traded in the bond market, but individual investors still are apt to be given less than the best prices to buy and sell Treasurys through brokers. To avoid paying any fees, the best way to buy Treasury bonds is through Treasury Direct, a program that allows you to buy side by side with the giant financial firms that bid on bonds at the Treasury's periodic auctions.

Treasury Direct is a very simple program, but it suffers, like most other government programs, from bureaucratic inertia. So don't plan on opening an account one day before the next scheduled auction. To get started, call your nearest Federal Reserve regional office (to find the one that serves you, see the list in the "Investor's Tool Kit" at the end of this book) or go to the Treasury's Web site at www.publicdebt.treas.gov to request a new account form (PDF 5182). It takes a few weeks for the account to be set up, but once it is the Treasury will debit your checking account (or you can send checks) for the amount of each bond you purchase at the auction. You will receive the same coupon rate as the big boys. But beware: If you decide you must sell your bond before it matures, you'll have to seek out a broker and take what he or she is willing to pay. The Treasury will handle the sale of three-month notes before they mature but will charge you a $34 fee for doing it, which takes a big chunk out of your earnings. The lesson: Buy and hold.

4

MONEY MANAGERS
AND MUTUAL FUNDS

As YOU BEGIN INVESTING, you'll find that suddenly everyone wants to help you get rich (including me). And we all want to be paid for doing it. It's just that some of us want to be paid a lot more than others. And some of us have better ways to help you get rich than others. Luckily for you, it turns out that the best way is also the cheapest way. That's because one of the biggest hurdles to getting rich is the cost of investing. The equation is simple: The higher the cost of investing, the less wealth your investments will produce. If I could find someone to whom I could pay huge sums of money to pick the perfect stocks for me day in and day out for the next forty years, I would gladly pay him or her 80 percent or 90 percent of my gains (I'd still be left with millions). But, as you'll discover, the financial services industry, by and large, doesn't want to work for a cut of your profits. Brokers, money managers, and mutual fund managers want to be paid regardless of whether you make money or lose it. There's a simple reason for that: None of them—absolutely none—can guarantee to make you richer every day for forty years. They can't—or at least won't—promise even to make you richer than you can make yourself by choosing some extraordinarily simple and low-cost investments. This chapter explains why I think the best of all worlds for investors is the broker-less world. My contention is that efficient markets—never mind exactly how efficient they are—make it futile not only for you and me to try to beat the market, but also for professional money managers working for the likes of Merrill Lynch and Fidelity to try to beat it. Yet brokers at Merrill Lynch and fund managers at Fidelity want you to pay them big bucks—which, by definition, hurts *your* return—to try to outperform the market consistently over a long period of time, a feat that extraordinarily few, if any, will be able to accomplish. And even though a few may achieve that goal, none of us can know in advance which lucky (that's all it is) few they will be. What it boils down to is that all those people who want to be paid for helping you invest are just hoping that they can make investing sound complicated and arcane enough that you won't notice the fees you're paying or the results you're getting. You'll just be grateful they're willing to take your money.

The financial services industry is one of the most persuasive forces on the face of the earth. Granted, it can persuade people to do only what they want to do. But given that most people want to make a lot of money, the fact that the financial services business offers myriad ways to do that makes the persuasion pretty easy. What I find particularly ironic is that the more wealth people amass, the more likely they are to seem to think they need help in turning it into even more wealth. I figure that anyone who can put together an investment portfolio worth upward of a million dollars or more is doing something right. Yet people I have known who have accomplished that feat—on their own—suddenly decide they need professional help. What I think they're really looking for is some psychological support. After all, a million dollars is a lot of money, and a mistake that costs you just 3 percent takes $30,000 off your portfolio's value. But 3 percent is about what money managers charge to manage your money for you, and for that you may get some hand-holding, but you're probably not going to get any real advice that you couldn't get elsewhere a lot cheaper. If anyone needs help from professionals, it's the person who can't figure out how to save enough to get a good running start at investing, and there are people out there—fee-only financial planners—whom I strongly endorse as sources of help for that kind of problem.

Less affluent or less enthusiastic investors, those who don't have the money to hire a manager or the time and energy to pursue stock picking on their own, find a compelling alternative in the mutual fund industry. Not only do funds offer instant diversification at relatively low cost (compared to money managers and full-service brokers), but they provide you, the investor, with a sense that someone who knows all about investing and finance is now in charge of your portfolio so you don't have to worry about making all those decisions about which stocks to buy and sell. All you have to do is worry about which funds to buy and sell, because there's always a new hot fund and always a new clunker that used to be hot. And while I've always thought of mutual funds as a way to avoid brokers and their commissions, the majority of funds are actually sold by brokers, whose commissions go a long way toward making it even more difficult for you to beat or even match the market's performance.

What I'm leading up to, of course, is what I think you should do to build and maintain your stock portfolio over the rest of your life: invest in index mutual funds. As I'll explain later, most—not all—of these funds have the exact characteristics a serious long-term investor needs: diversity, low cost, tax efficiency, and good service. It just doesn't get much better than that.

Now let me introduce you to the people who will soon try to become your best friend and financial confidant and will keep trying as long as you have a portfolio from which they can make their living.

BROKERS

I don't like stockbrokers. At least not the "full-service" kind. It isn't that they're bad people (although some are very, very bad indeed). Most of them are just trying to make a living. The trouble is, they're making their living by charging you for something that you're not getting: good advice. If you don't believe me, ask your broker for a list of five mutual funds you should buy. Chances are the list won't include any no-load mutual funds, the kind that don't charge any sales fee (from which a broker's commission is paid). Instead you'll get an explanation (I've heard this several times) about how no-load funds aren't really that good, that as in everything else, you get what you pay for. But take a look at those funds your broker recommends and see if you can't find five similar no-load funds that don't have better long-term records. The fact is, any broker who tells you that you get better performance from load funds than you get from no-load funds is telling a bald-faced lie. Your broker knows better, but there isn't any money for him or her in no-load funds. If everybody bought no-load funds, half the brokers in business today would have to find another line of work.

But brokers also advise their clients on which individual stocks or bonds to buy and sell. Since brokers tailor their sales pitch to each individual client, it's impossible to obtain any indication of how well a broker's recommendations have worked out except by being a guinea pig yourself. But you can be reasonably sure that an investor who works through a so-called full-service broker will wind up with, at best, a moderately good stock portfolio whose returns are much less than they should have been owing to high transaction costs and taxes. At worst, the portfolio assembled through the help of a broker will badly lag the market even before the extra costs of transaction fees and taxes are taken into account.

The reason for this, of course, is that the broker makes his or her income not from how well a portfolio performs, but from how many trades into and out of stocks and bonds the broker can persuade each client to make. The "advice" the broker offers about specific stocks or bonds arises from news events or "research reports" that suggest there may be a reason to buy or sell a particular stock or bond. But knowing as we do how efficient the markets are, you can be certain that the real professionals on trading desks and at the helm of big mutual funds will already have acted on any such news, leaving you and your broker to pick up their leavings. Seldom are the events the broker cites really sufficiently important to prompt a sale or purchase of a stock. To cap it all, the broker invariably will take credit for any stocks that rise, while blaming mysterious "market forces" for any losses you incur.

The securities industry is well aware of this problem, and many firms are trying to get around it by changing their brokers' stripes. They do this by seeking to imitate the broader services provided by money management firms, which I'll discuss shortly. The brokerage firms set up for an individual investor an all-encompassing account that can be called any number of fancy names but is known within the industry as a "wrap account." The generic name stems from the account's purpose, which is to wrap together various financial services, including cash management through a money market fund, as well as access to mutual funds and individual stocks and bonds. In many instances the investor is set up with a professional money manager (under the direction of the broker) who tailors a portfolio to suit the individual's circumstances. In exchange for such convenience, investors are expected to pay an annual fee of about 3 percent of the assets under management. Now, 3 percent is a lot to pay for stock advice alone, but to charge that kind of fee for basically putting an investor's money in a simple money market fund is outrageous. Beyond that, there are execution costs that add even more of a burden to the basic fee. In some instances the money manager must agree to funnel all trades through the sponsoring brokerage firm, which provides scant incentive for the manager to seek the lowest-cost sources for trading.

In some cases a broker may try to persuade an individual investor to get into a mutual fund wrap account that sports lower costs than a money management wrap account. But even then the costs are higher than they should be. In effect, such wrap accounts turn every mutual fund into a load fund regardless of whether or not the fund sponsor charges a load.

This isn't a blanket condemnation of all brokers. Brokers who merely take your orders to buy or sell individual stocks and don't try to generate commissions by persuading you to trade often are very useful if you want to buy and sell a few stocks on your own. But don't settle for anything but the lowest cost of execution. Discount brokers used to provide low-cost transactions, but they've been supplanted by "deep discount" brokers, who in turn have been challenged by on-line brokers for the lowest transaction costs. Be aware, though, that the heavily advertised bargain-basement fees you see are usually reserved for heavy traders. If you're just playing with a few stocks on the side occasionally while most of your money is in index funds and bonds (where I think it should be), you'll still be hit with uncomfortably high commissions from deep discount as well as on-line brokers. Another reason to live in a brokerless world.

MONEY MANAGERS

Money management firms have enjoyed a real boom in the last decade, and no wonder: a bull market in stocks coupled with an unprecedented period of innovation in technology and services has created a vast amount of wealth among entrepreneurs. The owners of much of that wealth are looking for help in managing it (or, about as often, in not losing it), and increasingly they're turning to money managers, who provide as much hand-holding to wealthy individuals as they do helpful advice. But that hand-holding comes at a cost. First, most money management firms set minimum amounts that they're willing to handle, ranging from around $50,000 for small firms operating in out-of-the-way cities and towns to $5 million at the most exclusive firms in places like New York, Los Angeles, and San Francisco. Then, once you're in the door, the fees start. The most basic is a fee of 3 percent or so charged on assets under management. Transaction fees can come on top of that, and other services, such as estate and trust planning, tax preparation, or the purchase or sale of property, bring additional fees. While there isn't a powerful incentive to trade their clients into and out of stocks and bonds frequently—particularly since many of their wealthy clients are more interested in preserving their wealth than in compounding it—I don't think the average money management firm, including the top-of-the-line private banks, performs any better than the average mutual fund manager, which is to say not as well as the overall market.

For investors with a few million dollars or more, the pampering received at a money management firm may be worth the price. After all, many of these people don't have the time or the inclination to take care of such trifling details as getting a will done or buying insurance, and they are typically accustomed to being deferred to by underlings, a role the typical money management firm fulfills well. But anyone with less than $1 million to invest probably isn't going to be using the ancillary services enough to make it worth paying the basic account fee. Better to put your money to work in a portfolio of low-cost stock mutual funds and hire the services of attorneys, tax preparers, or other advisers when and if they're needed.

FINANCIAL PLANNERS

If anyone in the financial services arena can be helpful to the average person, it's the financial planner. A financial planner's job is to help you determine what your financial goals are and how you can meet them. He or she will delve into your checkbook, bank statements, and investment accounts to determine what you're doing right—saving and investing, for example—and what you're doing wrong—eating out too often or buying too much life insurance. Then together you and the planner can work out a strategy aimed at improving your good financial habits while curbing your bad ones, all in the interest of reaching the goals you've described. But not all financial planners are created equal. The ones I favor are called "fee-only" financial planners. Logically that's because they make their money by charging you a fee, either on a per-hour basis or a flat fee for the development of a plan. Other planners may also charge a fee, but they tend to make the bulk of their money by selling you products that purportedly will help you reach your goals, products on which they, the planners, receive a commission. Now if I were a suspicious sort of guy, I might wonder if perhaps the plan these planners help cook up isn't weighted a little heavily toward products that produce the biggest commissions for the planner. Besides the likelihood that you're going to get unbiased help, the beauty of fee-only financial planners is that you can tap them only when you think you need them. Perhaps you'll use a planner just once in your life to help start you down the investing road, or maybe you'll go back from time to time to adjust your plan as your financial circumstances change. Some people schedule annual appointments with their planners for the reassurance of having an expert check on their progress. The point is, $150 or $200 or even $300 an hour for an expert, unbiased consultation may be worth the money if it helps you start and stick with a comprehensive investment program.

MUTUAL FUNDS

If stocks are the default choice for an investment portfolio, mutual funds are the default choice as a vehicle for buying and holding stocks. But not just any mutual funds. In fact, not the vast majority of mutual funds. We've already seen how brokers and money managers labor under the burden of high transaction costs and the virtual impossibility of providing superior long-term performance in efficient markets. Well, most mutual funds are in the same boat. No-load mutual funds—those that don't charge investors a sales commission—tend to have lower costs than money managers or brokers, but most don't have the *lowest* costs. Load mutual funds are simply not even in the ball game, although there are thousands of them and millions of investors buy them. And, of course, there is no reason to think that mutual fund managers are going to be any more successful in outperforming efficient markets than anyone else. That leaves us considering very few options within the mutual fund industry, and the ones that I think should be the ultimate default choice for most of your investment money are index funds. I'll explain more about their benefits (and shortcomings) a little further into the chapter. But it's worth knowing how various kinds of mutual funds work because you're going to be bombarded for the rest of your investing life from all directions by appeals to buy all sorts of funds. The better armed you are with knowledge, the less likely it is that you'll succumb to the expensive temptations laid before you.

Many of the millions of Americans who own mutual funds were introduced to them through their employers' retirement plans. Once they gained a basic familiarity with how funds work, these people began to put their savings outside of retirement plans into funds. And as the performance of various funds more or less mirrored the great bull market of the mid-1990s, ever more money poured into the funds. Indeed, one of the most popular (albeit flawed) indicators for predicting the future course of the stock market became the monthly statistics on how much money was flowing into funds (actually it was sort of a bimonthly statistic: first an educated guess soon after the end of a given month, followed a few weeks later by a more refined number). The rationale, of course, was that if money flowed into the fund companies, they would have to put it to work buying stocks, which would send stock prices higher. It didn't seem to occur to anyone that all that money might be *following* stock prices higher, rather than leading them. Only *after* the stock market swooned late in the summer of 1998 did the money flowing into stock mutual funds begin to drop off. Whatever the case, mutual funds enjoyed an immense popularity, and rightly so. Yet I'm afraid that the popularity, deserved as it might be, reflects more enthusiasm than knowledge, as evidenced by the fact that more money is invested in load funds than in no-load funds despite widespread evidence that such funds show absolutely no performance advantage over no-load funds. In fact, load funds lag the performance of no-load funds when the sales charges are taken into account. The truth is, investors who hold those funds have been suckered. No ifs, ands, or buts about it.

The recent popularity of mutual funds, and stocks in general, hasn't been subjected to a real test for many years. That will come in the next sustained bear market, when many funds will show negative results—perhaps severe losses—for a year or more. Nevertheless, mutual funds have been losing some of their luster recently. What has happened is that people are watching the incredible (some would say insane) performance of a few individual stocks (Internet stocks are a case in point) and despairing that they aren't earning those wildly outsize returns in their own mutual fund portfolio, never mind that the 20 percent–plus returns in many mutual funds during the last half of the 1990s were twice the average annual return for stocks. As a result we're seeing twenty-five-year-old investors without a clue as to how to analyze a stock and probably totally unaware of what it will cost them to trade a share of stock, setting out to outperform professional money managers. As long as the speculative mania surrounding such stocks continues, some of them may be able to do it. And their short-term results will tempt you to abandon funds and seek your own fortune among these superhot stocks. But I'm willing to bet that the investors who forgo the temptation and stick to mutual funds, especially index funds, will be in better financial shape ten, twenty, or thirty years from now than those gunslinging day traders they so envy right now. And they'll have wasted a lot less time doing it.

CLOSED-END AND OPEN-END FUNDS

There are basically two kinds of managed funds: closed-end and open-end. Since there are fewer of them and there are fewer reasons for owning them, I'll get closed-end funds out of the way first. The name derives from the fact that once the number of shares to be issued by the fund is determined, the fund is effectively closed to the creation of new shares. The sale of those original shares raises the money that is then invested in securities selected to achieve the fund's aims. After the initial public offering of closed-end fund shares, the shares are listed for trading on an exchange. If an investor wants to own those shares, they must be purchased from someone who wants to sell them.

This supply-and-demand aspect of closed-end funds results in a curious discrepancy: the price of a share of the fund may be (and usually is) worth more or less than the value of the assets it represents. Let's say a closed-end fund has been created to invest in companies in South Korea, a country that has been less than hospitable to individual foreign investors but invites institutional investors, such as closed-end funds. The fund sells one million shares of what we'll call the SK Fund for $10 each, raising $10 million. Of that $10 million, we'll say $100,000 is siphoned off by the management company as a commission, leaving $9.9 million to invest in South Korean stocks (that means, of course, that your $10 share, had you bought in the IPO, is immediately worth just $9.90). Once the fund owns those stocks, it can calculate each day a "net asset value" (NAV), which is the total value of the South Korean securities divided by the number of shares outstanding. For this hypothetical example we'll assume South Korean stocks remain unchanged for a period of time and the NAV of SK Fund shares holds steady at $9.90. But if something occurs that persuades some original shareholders that they don't want to own South Korean stocks (North Korea threatens to invade, for example), they'll have to find someone else to buy their SK Fund shares. Since SK Fund shares aren't that attractive now that invasion is threatened, the best bid the sellers might get could be $8 a share. The original buyer of SK Fund shares has now lost $2 (not counting sales commissions from his or her broker), and the new buyer now owns $9.90 of assets for just $8.

The hypothetical example illustrates some important aspects that make closed-end funds undesirable investments: The shares almost always sell at a premium to the NAV in the initial public offering and usually trade at a discount soon afterward. While it might seem reasonable to buy $9.90 of assets for $8, the trouble is that the discount could worsen, so you wind up owning shares that you can sell for only $7, even though the NAV remains $9.90. On occasion, closed-end fund prices rise above the NAV (they are said to sell at a premium). If you bought such a fund at a discount and it rose to a premium, you would be very happy (assuming you sold your shares at a premium). But if you buy a closed-end fund at a premium, you are indeed pursuing the "greater fool" theory of investing, assuming someone even dumber than you will come along and pay a higher premium. The majority of closed-end funds are aimed at buying and holding a specific state's municipal bonds to gain tax advantages. Closed-end stock funds tend to be aimed at investing in specific countries or regions of the world, although closed-end funds exist that aim at certain sectors of the stock market, such as health and biotechnology or science and technology.

Open-end funds (the technical name for what most of us call mutual funds) are just what the name implies: funds that are open to the creation of new shares at any time. If you want to buy into an open-end fund, simply send the fund your money and you'll receive new shares created at whatever the NAV is on the day your money arrives. The fund manager then applies your money to buying more shares or bonds of the kind the fund wants to own. Should you sell your shares, you'll be paid whatever the NAV is at the end of the day on which you ask to redeem. The fund manager will, in effect, simply sell a representative sample of stocks or bonds the fund owns to raise the cash you're paid. Actually, most funds keep a little cash lying around to meet redemptions without having to sell shares, a useful practice for them but one that doesn't really help investors who want their money to be put to work in stocks, not cash reserves. All other things being equal, I think open-end funds are far superior to closed-end funds as investment vehicles. But there are dozens of kinds of open-end funds, and even within single categories they certainly are not created equal. We'll start with the safe and simple funds, then work our way through the riskier and more complex types of funds available to investors.

MONEY MARKET FUNDS

Money market funds are the simplest of the open-end funds to understand and are a wonderful illustration of why mutual funds are so useful to individual investors. Money market funds give individuals access to an investment class that would otherwise be beyond their reach, and they provide better returns than competing investments. Both individual and institutional investors frequently use money market funds as a parking place for cash that is intended to be used for something else later, and you should consider doing the same. While not as absolutely safe as a government-insured checking or savings account at a bank, money market funds have a superb record, and the yields are considerably higher than those of bank accounts without any significant loss of liquidity (most money market funds offer check-writing privileges for amounts in excess of certain low minimums).

"Money market" is a generic term that covers what pros call the market for government and corporate "paper," which is short-term (usually less than six months) loans that help governments and companies manage their cash flow. Few companies are interested in going to all the trouble to borrow money for the short term from individual investors; the marketing and administrative costs would be prohibitive. And, of course, few individuals would be interested in the time and trouble it would take to manage such short-term investments, including the frequent reinvestment decisions that would be required as the short-term loans were repaid. So companies deal with institutional investors, such as banks, insurance companies, and money market funds, all of which can assemble large amounts of money quickly and efficiently.

As a money market investor, you and thousands of other investors pool your money, which is then lent at a competitive rate. As with any such transaction, the rate is determined by the relative risk of the loan: the U.S. Treasury can pay less for a loan than General Electric, and GE pays less than a small company that's having trouble paying its bills. There are, however, a number of restrictions imposed by the Securities and Exchange Commission on what kinds of investments a money market fund can make. A money market fund is limited in the duration of its investments: the average maturity cannot exceed ninety days. As we learned in chapter 3, the longer the term of a loan, the more the risk that interest rates may move unfavorably. With maturities of under ninety days, interest rate risk is minimal. What's more, money market funds are restricted to dealing with creditworthy entities: government agencies (including state and municipal governments) and high-rated corporate borrowers. Companies that don't make that cut must deal with insurance companies, banks, or other lenders to obtain short-term loans. Because of these restrictions, the opportunities for one money market fund to outperform another by a wide margin are rare (although it is true that, on average, a money market fund lending to corporate borrowers will have a higher yield than one lending only to government entities).

Can you, then, pick a money market fund at random and expect to achieve the same yield?

Not by a long shot. Because of the competitive nature of the market and the restrictions on the type of investments they can make, money market funds illustrate better than anything else a central point about investing: Costs matter. How well a fund company runs its operations and how it passes along its costs of doing business to investors are often ignored but critical components of fund investing. Let's take as an example two money market funds that invest in U.S. Treasury securities. The gross yields (before expenses) on those securities as issued by the Treasury will vary only slightly, depending on the average maturity and date of purchase by the two funds. We'll give Fund A a gross yield of 3.17 percent annually and Fund B a gross yield of 3.12 percent. But let's also assume that Fund B takes pains to control its costs of doing business, while Fund A is more lackadaisical about costs. Fund A has an expense ratio of .54 percent (that's what it charges you and other fund holders for its services). Back that .54 percent out of the 3.17 percent gross yield, and the net yield to you is 2.63 percent. Fund B, on the other hand, has an expense ratio of .33 percent and thus provides you with a net yield of 2.79 percent. The difference doesn't seem like much, but if you know anything about compounding, you know that a penny saved today becomes quite a few more pennies over years of compounding. I'm totally convinced that in the realm of money market funds, picking the fund with the lowest costs among its peers will do more to improve your returns than any other step you can take.

One caution should be raised, however. While the yields from money market funds will almost certainly be higher than what can be obtained from bank savings accounts, the yield on a money market account is not predictable. The yield changes as market conditions change. While yields have soared as high as 15 percent during periods of high inflation in the early 1980s, they have recently settled between 3.5 percent and 5 percent, depending on the type of fund, with a slow trend downward due to quiescent inflation.

BOND FUNDS

The concept of bond funds seems eminently simple: A fund manager buys a bunch of bonds and then passes along the interest payments and any capital gains (minus a management fee) to all the fund holders. Yet the world of bond funds is just as complex as that of stock funds. On the first level is the duration of a bond fund: short-, intermediate-, or long-term. Each of those categories has its own characteristics. Then comes the question of creditworthiness (or risk). The range extends from U.S. Treasury and government agency bonds through high-grade corporate issues to high-yield (I call them by their more appropriate name, junk) and emerging market bond funds. Finally, an investor must address the question of taxation: taxable or tax-exempt? With all those choices, one begins to gain an appreciation of how difficult it can be to select a bond fund.

The solution that I favor is to simply say "no" to all the above. The reason for such a simple solution lies in my conviction that stocks are the best vehicle for *amassing* wealth through investing. Bonds, and specifically Treasury bonds, on the other hand, are the best vehicles for *protecting* wealth. Bond funds, however, are not the same thing as bonds. Unlike a bond, which has a definite maturity date, a bond fund has no maturity date. And because a fund is continually adding to its portfolio of bonds and sometimes selling part of its holdings to be replaced by other bonds, a bond fund incurs transaction expenses and capital gains taxes (fans of tax-free municipal bond funds often conveniently overlook the fact that while their interest payment is tax-free, any capital gains resulting from trading by the fund manager are fully taxable at the appropriate rate). The interest paid by the fund varies according to the maturity and yield of the bonds the fund holds. Finally, because interest rate fluctuations affect the value of bonds held in a fund's portfolio, the value of a share of the portfolio fluctuates as well. The net result of all these factors is that the certainty that comes with owning a bond directly disappears when an investor buys a bond fund instead. More to the point, that loss of certainty isn't accompanied by a commensurate rise in expected returns.

However, I'll be the first to admit that some types of bond funds behave better than others and thus are more suitable for investors willing to trade certainty for potential—note I said "potential"—gains. The best example I can think of is the substitution of a short-term bond fund for the money market accounts we discussed in the previous section of this chapter. No doubt about it, money market funds offer better than bank account yields with a high degree of liquidity and the comfort of a fixed price of $1 a share. But if an investor is willing to trade a little of that comfort and liquidity, a short-term bond fund can provide a worthwhile extra yield. It is true that the NAV of the fund's shares may rise or fall with the direction of overall interest rates, but because of the relatively short maturity (two to four years, typically) of the bonds held by the fund, that price change will usually be insignificant. And if an investor sticks to funds that invest in short-term government bonds, the risk of default is nonexistent.

Once you are past short-term government bond funds, however, the picture begins to get more complicated and grows increasingly risky as funds extend their maturity and reach further down the creditworthiness scale to capture bigger yields. We've already examined in chapter 3 how the prices of long-term bonds fluctuate more markedly than short-term bonds. The same is true of long-term bond funds. As overall interest rates rise and fall in response to inflation fears and other factors, the NAVs of long-term bond funds rise and fall faster than the NAVs of intermediate- and short-term funds. That may not matter if you are seeking only the income stream from a bond fund and are certain that you won't need to sell your fund shares, which may drop substantially below the price you paid for them if interest rates rise. Creditworthiness counts, too. While it is true that lower-rated bonds pay higher yields, there's a reason for that: The risk of default is higher. All it takes is a few defaults within a bond fund's portfolio for the value of that fund's shares to drop significantly (while money market funds are able to cover such sins by making up the difference from their own income). In times of uncertainty, the prices of riskier bonds will always drop faster and further than those of safe bonds with the same maturities. That's why by the time you begin considering high-yield and emerging market bond funds, you're getting into investment vehicles that behave as much like stocks as bonds without the long-term returns that stocks offer. Why not just own stocks?

In any event, if you are shopping for a bond fund, there are several points to keep in mind, not the least of which is that costs matter. Any two bond funds that invest in substantially similar bonds (say, Treasury bonds with an average maturity of twelve years) will produce gross yields that are nearly similar because the bond market (at the institutional level, not at the individual investor level) is efficient. Given that similarity, it is a simple matter to conclude that the fund with the lower expenses will provide an investor with a superior return.

But operating expenses aren't the only consideration. Bond fund managers can goose their funds' yields through a variety of stratagems that might not be obvious if you look only at the yield. For example, a bond fund can be classified as intermediate-term if its average maturity ranges anywhere from seven to ten years. But a fund with an average maturity of ten years will tend to have a higher yield than a fund with an average maturity of seven years. Of course, it will also exhibit more price volatility. So before leaping at the higher-yielding fund among the many in any given category, find out about average maturity (it will be in the prospectus).

Within some kinds of funds, the quality of the bonds that make up the portfolio can vary, too. Corporate bond funds, for example, can enhance their yield by increasing the ratio of lower-rated bonds in the portfolio, but only at the risk of greater default and higher price volatility.

Finally, there are funds that use derivative products to try to boost their yields. Some government agency bond funds, for example, may use collateralized mortgage obligations (CMOs) to increase their yield. CMOs are essentially pools of mortgages that have been sliced and diced to provide a variety of securities, some of which represent payment of the principal on the mortgages, some of which represent payment of just the mortgage interest, and others that are combinations of principal and interest. The trouble, as we saw in chapter 3, is that it is exceedingly difficult to predict when mortgages will be repaid, so the returns from these funds can vary widely and unpredictably—sort of like stocks, but without the long-term returns. So again, why not buy stocks instead?

Before leaving the subject of bond funds, you need to think about your tax status. I know it isn't fun, but it could be lucrative. Among the offerings of the mutual fund industry are bond funds that allow you to avoid paying some or all taxes on the income you earn. At the simplest level, income from U.S. Treasury bonds, whether received directly from a bond or through a bond fund that invests in Treasury issues, is exempt from state and local taxes. For fortunate fund holders who live in places with no state income tax, that feature is essentially meaningless. But for those who live in states with punishingly high tax rates, such as New York or New Jersey, the exemption from those taxes on Treasury bond income can help close the gap between the yield paid by Treasury funds and that paid by riskier corporate bond funds.

More broadly, there are many bond funds that invest principally in tax-exempt municipal bonds. Like the bonds themselves, these funds pay a lower yield than other kinds of bonds. But if you are in the higher tax brackets, those funds can provide you with a superior after-tax return, albeit at a higher risk if you're comparing them with Treasury bond funds. Finally, a more recent innovation is single-state tax-exempt funds, whose purpose is obvious: to make income totally free from federal, state, and local taxes. Of course, they work only in states with income taxes, but in places like New York and New Jersey they can be particularly useful. Just remember that by holding a single-state bond fund, you're putting an unduly high concentration of your money in the hands of local and state politicians. Knowing what I do about New York and New Jersey politicians, I'd rather spread my wealth around. You'll have to make your own judgments about the political picture in your state and whether it's worth the risk of gaining somewhat higher after-tax returns.

In the end, taking into account all the various factors that affect bond funds, and assuming that you're seeking income and not capital gains from a fund, my recommendation is to stick with the inflation-indexed Treasury bonds discussed in the bond chapter. An alternative, if your tax situation clearly justifies the extra risk, would be tax-exempt national funds. My own opinion is that investing in anything else is simply trading too much risk for too little extra income.

STOCK FUNDS: PAST PERFORMANCE
IS NO INDICATOR OF FUTURE PERFORMANCE

Okay, we've gotten the minor stuff out of the way. Now it's time to examine the one category of mutual funds that serious long-term investors will find most useful: open-end stock mutual funds. Most of us who buy stock mutual funds are looking for one thing: superior gains. To achieve that goal, we diligently study the daily, monthly, and quarterly mutual fund scorecards in *The Wall Street Journal*, we snap up whichever of the financial advice magazines promises to reveal to us the "Five Best Mutual Funds to Buy Now!" and we constantly swap out of our old funds and into the funds that just scored big in the latest monthly or quarterly performance lists.

All, unfortunately, to little avail. Indeed, by chasing performance, we actually diminish it through the taxes we pay each time we sell one fund to buy another.

I've said it before and I'll say it again: There isn't any evidence that you or anyone else can know in advance which of the many funds out there will outperform all the others. The funds themselves warn you (regulators make them; they certainly wouldn't do it otherwise) that past performance is no indication of future performance, and since past performance is about all we have on which to base a decision to switch from one fund to another, the whole process seems doomed to failure.

Does that mean you should simply throw up your hands and turn away from funds?

Not at all.

What it does mean is that you need to understand the value of mutual funds. They aren't a competitive game in which you have to own better-performing funds each month or quarter than your neighbors or colleagues. Rather, they are tools to be used to help you create wealth. Stock mutual funds provide some things that most of us can't afford to obtain any other way. The most obvious benefit is diversification. Diversification of a stock portfolio is as much a safety device as a technique for wealth creation. Diversification would make no sense if someone knew which stock would rise the most over some period of time. To buy anything but that stock would result in a reduced return. But since no one knows which stock that will be, an investor takes a risk by holding just one stock. While it might go up, it might also go down, and by a substantial amount. If we hold two stocks instead of one, we reduce the risk that a single stock might plummet and wipe out our wealth. The more stocks in the portfolio, the less danger any one poses to the value of the portfolio. Of course, the downside is that the more stocks you own, the less likely it will be that any single one that rises will contribute significantly to the growth of the portfolio. That's why so many individual investors, trying to strike it rich, have woefully undiversified portfolios. They're simply betting that they've picked the right stock. Their chances of having done that are only slightly better than their chances of winning the lottery.

Buying a diversified portfolio of individual stocks costs money. The most efficient way to purchase stocks is in round lots of one hundred shares. If we assume the average price of a stock is $30, that means it will take $3,000 plus commissions to put one stock in a portfolio. To obtain reasonable diversification, we would probably want at least twenty-five stocks in a portfolio, which means that to set up the most basic portfolio would require $75,000, plus commissions. Shares of mutual funds that afford much more diversification than that can be had for as little as $250.

The Simple Solution: Index Funds

But the number and kinds of open-end stock funds that confront an investor can be bewildering at first. Relax. As I pointed out at the beginning of this chapter, I wouldn't come near the majority of funds that are offered, and neither should you. It's relatively easy to pare the list down to a manageable size once you set some criteria by which to make your selections. The result of that whittling away process invariably comes down to one answer: index funds. A list of the stock index funds that I consider the world's best (and a list of the second best) can be found in the "Investor's Tool Kit" at the back of this book.

The first and easiest criterion is cost. What will it cost you to buy and own shares of a given fund? The answer is clearly "Too much" if you consider any funds that charge sales commissions, or "loads." These extra charges usually come in the form of "front-end loads," which are paid at the time of purchase, but there are also "back-end loads," which are charged when a fund's shares are sold. Loads tend to be around 5 percent of the amount invested and, to be fair, are onetime charges. In other words, if you buy a fund with a 5 percent load and sell it one year later, your average annual return will be reduced by 5 percent. But if you sell the fund after five years, the load will have reduced the average annual return by 1 percent and over ten years by just .5 percent. Still, any diminution of performance through loads is money that has simply been thrown away. The only reason ever to pay a load is to get guaranteed superior performance. Since no one can guarantee that performance, there isn't any need to pay a load. Paying a commission does nothing but set up an exra hurdle to the achievement of superior or even average gains in a mutual fund.

But loads are only one of the many costs mutual fund investors face. A more onerous (because it is imposed every year, not just once) and equally unjustifiable charge is the so-called 12b-1 fee, which some funds charge shareholders to offset the cost of marketing the fund. The rationale behind the fee is that by expanding the size of the fund, all shareholders will benefit from the economies of scale that come with a larger operation. But more often than not, the economies that are realized through running a larger organization are far smaller than the size of the 12b-1 fees. Instead, a chunk of those 12b-1 fees go right into the pockets of the fund sponsors. If such deceit isn't irritating enough, consider the case of funds that have grown so fast, the managers can't keep up with the massive inflows of money and decide to close the fund to new investors yet continue to charge 12b-1 fees that are intended to bring in more new investors.

Once you get past loads and 12b-1 fees—what I call "illegitimate expenses," since they do essentially nothing to help the investor—you come to legitimate expenses: investment advisory fees and administrative costs. But just because they're legitimate—that is, the fund couldn't operate without charging them—doesn't mean they can't be excessive. Investment advisory fees, or management fees, are paid to the people who actually make the investment decisions and maintain the fund. Part of the management fee pays the commissions on trades and other activities directly related to the creation and maintenance of the portfolio, and the rest is profit for the managers. Administrative costs cover the expenses related to maintaining accounts and records and executing transactions requested by shareholders. And it's these fees where index funds tend to shine for several reasons. One is that an index fund manager is seldom a "star" in the mutual fund world whose name is instantly recognized by individual investors. Those stars, who are benefiting from a winning streak that garners them immense amounts of publicity, can command huge salaries and bonuses (which come right out of the fund's results) because they draw so many individual investors to their funds. That isn't to say that index fund managers aren't well paid for their services, which, as we'll see momentarily, are a lot more complicated than you probably think.

Then there's the matter of transaction costs. Many active fund managers, in their quest to beat the market, shift rapidly from one sector of the market to another and frenetically trade stocks within those sectors to lock in gains or to cut losses. While it is true the big funds can command extremely low per-share trading costs, even those low costs amount to considerable sums when the fund's portfolio turns over 100 percent or more per year (a 100 percent turnover implies that the fund didn't hold any of its stocks more than a year). But an index fund needs to execute trades only as new money comes into the fund or old money leaves it and when the stock components of the target index change. Thus index funds have very low transaction costs compared with those of the active managers who are trying to beat the index.

Before we leave the subject of costs, a word to the unwary: Not all stock funds are created equal, and neither are all index funds. While it strikes me as the height of irresponsibility (by both the sponsors of the funds and the investors who buy them), there are index funds that have high management costs and even a few that charge loads. So don't assume that just because a fund advertises itself as an index fund, it will automatically be no-load and low expense. "Ever vigilant" is a good motto for any investor to adopt.

There are fees, called "transaction fees," that I consider justifiable and, indeed, good for long-term investors. The fee basically goes to make up for the costs of buying and selling shares. By charging the individual investor a modest fee each time he or she invests new money, the fund avoids imposing that particular transaction cost on all the other shareholders. If you're a long-term investor, the fee shouldn't bother you since it's designed to discourage short-term investors, who otherwise can drive up transaction costs for everyone. The fee is typically charged by funds that invest in securities that aren't particularly liquid, such as small stocks and foreign stocks.

All these costs can be found by a close reading of a fund's prospectus. It's easy enough to weed out funds that charge a load, but to get a true picture of the costs of owning a fund beyond that requires a little study. Lest you think that determining the costs isn't important, consider a study done a few years ago that showed that the annual cost of holding the most expensive funds averaged about 3.5 percent per year, while the cost of the least expensive funds ran just 0.4 percent annually. That 2.9 percent may not sound like much when many funds are returning 18 percent or more per year, but it could mean the difference in profits or losses in the next bear market and will surely be noticeable even when the stock market returns to its average 11 percent or so annual returns. Certainly it will have a profound effect on your results over the next twenty or thirty years as compounding widens even tiny differences in performance. Thus, all other things being equal, the fund with the lowest costs should command your attention.

While costs apparently don't get much consideration by most investors (mutual funds with loads would disappear otherwise), performance, particularly short-term performance, is probably the single variable that most fund investors use to make decisions about where to invest. And that's unfortunate, because it results in needless time, energy, and money spent in what usually is a futile quest. Look at it this way: If you choose to chase performance (and you can only chase it, you can't get ahead of it with any certainty), you almost certainly will wind up dumping one fund to buy another. The fund you dump will either have been profitable for you, in which case you'll owe taxes on the gain, or it will have lost money for you, in which case you're locking in your loss. Both moves will hurt your ultimate performance. Even if you avoid the temptation to buy or sell funds based on the latest quarterly performance statistics, you'll still face the need to make buy and sell decisions eventually if you own actively managed funds. That's because the performance of actively managed funds is usually attributed (rightly or wrongly) to the manager's expertise. But managers are human: they can be lured away by another fund company if they're good, or they can retire or even die. When the manager you thought was responsible for your good performance departs from the fund you own (and almost all will over the thirty or forty years you'll be investing), you will have to decide if the new manager will be as good. If you think not, then you've got to sell and look for another fund to buy, again triggering taxes on your gains (presumably you dumped any losing fund a long time before the manager was fired).

Index funds avoid the need for that kind of decision making (and the resulting costs, in the form of either taxes or locked-in losses). There are two important points to understand about index fund performance. The first is that to the extent an index represents a market, the performance of the index represents the average performance of all investors—mutual fund managers, pension fund managers, hotshot traders, and individual investors. As with any average, some of the players will have done better and some will have done worse. But that's before expenses. The performance of the target index itself represents pure performance because there are no costs—no commissions to buy and sell stocks and no managers to pay—while the performance of any investor must reflect costs. So if half the investors do better than the index with their stock picking and half worse before costs, more than half will always underperform the index once costs are taken into account. The second point is that while index fund managers may come and go, there will seldom be any difference in the performance of the fund. Assuming the new manager is competent, the index fund will continue to reflect the performance of the target index. Thus an investor can choose when to sell shares based entirely on his or her own needs and not on some extraneous influence like the departure of the fund manager. It's easy to imagine buying and holding index fund shares for decades; only the most foolish investors will assume that they can buy and hold actively managed funds for anything like that period of time if they have any reason to believe fund managers make a difference to performance. And what other reason would they have to buy the fund in the first place if they didn't believe that?

While we've already discussed the cost advantage that well-run index funds should have over actively managed funds, there's another cost factor that is unique to each individual investor:

taxes. All stock mutual funds, including index funds, wind up sell-ing some of the shares of stock they hold each year. Index funds sell shares because some shareholders want to take their money out or because of changes in the structure of the target index. But the typical active manager, always trying to beat the market by moving nimbly from one sector to another, sells a lot more of his or her stocks than does the typical index fund manager. The result of all that selling is to trigger capital gains (hopefully investors flee any funds whose selling triggers lots of losses), which are passed on to the fund's shareholders as distributions. The gains paid to share-holders are then taxed (assuming they aren't held in tax-advantaged 401(k) plans or individual retirement accounts) at the individual's marginal income tax rate. For short-term gains that means that a taxpayer living in New York or New Jersey and pay-ing at the highest federal rates loses something like 50 percent of the value of those gains in taxes. While the fund's performance statistics may look fine in the prospectus or in the newspaper stock tables, your actual performance may differ considerably once you've taken into account your tax bill. And, of course, it's surpris-ing and dismaying to find late in the year (when funds typically pay their distributions) that you've suddenly got several thousand dollars of taxable income for which you've made no provision for withholding. The point is that while any fund can produce such unpleasant surprises, index funds tend to be far more tax efficient than actively managed funds. The official performance statistics don't reflect that efficiency, but your checkbook certainly will.

Do you want to invest in stocks, or do you want to hold cash? If your answer is stock, then index funds are again your first choice. The reason: Active money managers often try to time the market, keeping some cash lying around to take advantage of dips or as a result of taking profits at what they think are market peaks. The trouble is, they aren't any better at timing the markets than the rest of us. As a result, in an overall rising market like the one we've had in the United States, any money sitting idly by and not invested in stocks hurts performance. Index funds, by their very nature, must be fully invested at all times if they're to have any hope of matching their target index.

Idle cash lying around many funds is just one manifestation of a bigger problem among actively managed funds: not getting what you think you're getting. When you buy a mutual fund it should be with a conscious intention to accomplish some objective. If you buy an aggressive growth fund, for instance, you should get a fund that invests in aggressive growth stocks. And if you want a small-cap fund, you should get a fund that owns small-cap stocks. I admit that over the past few years the mutual fund industry has gotten a little better about hewing to its purported aims. But that came only after what was then the nation's largest stock fund, Fidelity's Magellan, surprised many of its investors by investing heavily in the U.S. bond market. Investors who bought Magellan shares thought they were buying a premier growth stock fund, not a partial bond fund. They might have been forgiving had the bet on bonds worked out well, but it didn't. It was a disaster that badly hurt Magellan's returns and reputation. The manager who pulled that stunt left not long afterward. There are still actively managed funds that advertise themselves as one thing but in reality do something different, and it's often difficult to find out which ones they are until after the fact. With an index fund you know you're getting what you're seeking: the target index is usually well defined and easy for you to track. It isn't likely the fund manager will be able to stray much at all from his or her assigned task of matching as closely as possible the performance of that target.

Since an index fund manager can't deviate much from his or her assigned task, and because that task seems relatively simple, it occurs to many investors that a monkey could run a stock index fund. Professional management? Come on, they say, how hard can it be to duplicate a index's performance?

"Plenty hard" is the answer. Think back to our earlier discussion about costs. An index fund manager is constantly striving to match the performance of an index that itself doesn't pay salaries, administrative overhead, or any of the other expenses that typically sap a mutual fund's performance. What's more, the index itself doesn't have to deal with fickle investors who throw millions at it one day, then turn around and draw millions out the next day. And unlike their colleagues who manage active funds, index managers can't afford to keep around a pot full of cash, since every dollar held in cash detracts from matching the performance of the target index.

Because money is always flowing into and out of funds, index fund managers have to be particularly nimble in putting new money to work. They also have to buy and sell dozens of stocks in the right mix to duplicate the performance of their target index. And when whoever runs the real index decides to change some components, index fund managers have to scramble to unload the stocks that leave the index and replace them with the ones that are being added. The best index fund managers—performance differences are measured in hundredths of a percentage point—are particularly adept at buying and selling futures contracts, which give them the right to buy or sell an index's stocks at a set time and price.

Occasionally the savvy use of futures contracts allows an index fund manager to actually beat his or her target index. But the truth is, most index funds will wind up lagging slightly behind their target index. But then again, so do most active managers. And active management costs investors a lot more.

Now, I freely admit that there are some psychological hurdles to becoming an index fund fan. By far the largest is that a decision to use index funds requires the admission by the investor that he or she no longer will attempt to beat the market but will consent to take whatever performance the market, as measured by the chosen index, will deliver. You will never see an S&P index fund leading the best-performance charts in *The Wall Street Journal*. But—and this is the point—your fund's returns will almost certainly beat those of the majority of actively managed funds over a period of five years or more. And you will never see an S&P index fund at the bottom of *The Wall Street Journal* performance charts, either.

While S&P 500 funds are by far the most popular index funds, there are funds available to take you just about anywhere you want to go. You can, for instance, take the one-stop shopping approach and buy a total market fund that reflects the overall performance of the entire U.S. stock market. Or you can slice and dice the market up into components, buying large-cap stocks through an S&P index fund and supplementing that with midcap and small-cap index funds. You can even divide further and specialize in buying the value (low P/E) or growth (high P/E) portions of small-, mid-, or large-cap index funds. And although I'm not particularly enamored of bond funds, there are index bond funds that make a lot of sense if you want to go the bond fund route because they sport the lowest costs. And given the lower overall returns of bonds, costs become even more critical to long-term performance.

INDEX FUND ALTERNATIVES:
EXCHANGE-TRADED FUNDS

While index mutual funds have been around for years and have been growing in popularity as investors come to understand their many advantages, a relatively new kind of indexed investment has been growing much more rapidly: "exchange-traded funds" (ETFs). These are a form of unit investment trust (UIT), an investment vehicle that has been around for years and has mostly been used to buy bonds. In the bond world a UIT is nothing more than a pool of bonds in which investors buy shares. A trust is formed, sells its shares, and then throws off periodic income to its shareholders until the bonds in the pool mature. The latest wrinkle in unit investment trusts involves setting up a pool of stocks that produce returns duplicating those of the S&P 500, the Dow Jones Industrial Average, the NASDAQ 100, or even some foreign stock market indexes. They're exactly like an index fund in that they duplicate the performance of their target index at a low cost. They differ, however, in that their shares are traded directly on a stock exchange (mostly on the American Stock Exchange, where their popularity has brought a failing exchange back from near oblivion). When you buy a mutual fund you can place your order anytime you want to, but you'll buy the fund at the net asset value calculated after trading is over for the day. With exchange-traded index funds, the price of the fund is calculated constantly as the stock prices within it change. Further, it can be bought as a "market order" (at whatever is the price prevailing on the floor of the exchange when the order is received) or as a "limit order" (good only if the price of the trust hits a predetermined value). And, like stocks, ETFs can be bought on "margin" (with borrowed money) and can even be "shorted" (you borrow ETF shares and sell them, hoping to buy them back later at a lower price, thus making a profit on the difference).

The marketing behind these products has been clever. The S&P 500 product, for example, is formally called a Standard & Poor's depositary receipt, but it trades under the easily remembered symbol SPY and is popularly called a Spider. And shares of the Dow Jones Industrial Average ETF trade under the symbol DIA and are called Diamonds. The expense ratio of these products can be very low. Spiders recently had an expense ratio of 0.12 percent, well below the 0.18 percent of Vanguard's S&P 500 index fund, often regarded as the benchmark of low-cost fund investing. And the fact that they can be traded instantly at a known price certainly adds to their popularity. In just the last year, that popularity has soared. Even Vanguard, that bastion of conservative mutual fund investing, joined the party by offering its own ETF product.

One question then arises: Are these products a better long-term bet than regular index funds? If you intend to follow the precepts in this book, probably not. First, let's consider the ability to trade into and out of index funds quickly, to buy them on margin, and to short them. Why do you want to be able to do any of those things? It doesn't surprise me that the NASDAQ 100 Trust, an ETF traded under the symbol QQQ and known as Cubes, quickly became wildly popular after its introduction in 1999. Recall that the NASDAQ is home to huge numbers of technology companies, and the NASDAQ 100 index sports some of the best-known names in technology, including Microsoft, Intel, and Hewlett-Packard, as well as some of the fastest-growing companies. That rapid rise in popularity was merely a reflection of thousands of traders leaping into and out of the NASDAQ 100 rather than into and out of many of the individual stocks that it comprises. In other words, it was "hot" money taking advantage of what seemed yet another opportunity to make a fast buck. If you count yourself among that group, then sure, the exchange-traded funds might work for you. But if you're a buy-and-hold investor—the only kind there should be, it seems to me—then you simply don't need the liquidity of these products. Whether you buy your shares of an index fund at $95 at the end of the day or $94.98 (or $95.25) during the day isn't going to make a lot of difference to your results twenty-five years from now.

Second, think about the costs. Sure, the Spider's expense ratio may be lower than even the best index fund's ratio, but that doesn't include your own transaction costs. To buy exchange-traded funds, you're going to have to pay a broker to get in and, eventually, to get back out. And if you don't trade often, it is highly unlikely that you're going to qualify for any of those superlow commissions you see advertised by many brokers. So here you are buying an index fund on which you're essentially paying a load. Certainly if you adopt a dollar cost–averaging approach to making your fund investments, it will be difficult for the exchange-traded products, with their brokerage fees attached to every periodic purchase you make, to come in under the cost of buying, owning, and selling a similar mutual fund.

But there are real advantages to the popularity of ETFs. The main one—and one of the reasons Vanguard found it useful to set up its own ETFs—is that they will probably draw away much of the "hot" money that formerly dashed into and back out of standard open-end index funds. That means the managers of those funds can run them more efficiently, with fewer transaction costs and realized capital gains. And for those of us who remain in the staid old index funds, that means better returns. Not a bad deal, is it?

PART TWO

PORTFOLIOS FOR LONG-TERM INVESTORS

5

UNDERSTANDING RISK AND RETURN

YOU NOW KNOW about the superior long-term performance of stocks over other investments. You know about the advantages of low-cost index funds that match the market. You know about the tempering effects of reliable income from inflation-indexed government bonds. And you know what a huge difference it makes to be able to save and invest new money constantly. Now it's time to put it all together and figure out what to do with that knowledge.

If this were an ordinary book about investing, this section would be all about "asset allocation." And don't get me wrong, asset allocation is an extremely important concept for long-term investors. How you distribute (allocate) your money (assets) among various investment options is actually more important to your long-term success as an investor than picking the right stocks, bonds, or mutual funds. In other words, having 80 percent of your money in stocks (either individual stocks or mutual funds) is much more important to your eventual success than if you carefully picked each stock and each fund but had only 75 percent of your money in stocks. But rather than get into an esoteric discussion about what the right mix is for any given investor (that answer is "It depends"), I'm going to construct some hypothetical portfolios demonstrating the various ways in which all the information we've discussed so far can be put to work to build a portfolio tailored to your specific goals, finances, and stage of life. The portfolios are designed primarily to be helpful to people in each age bracket who are just starting a serious investment program. But there are lessons in each age group that can be applied to younger or older investors as well. While I discuss building these portfolios as means to reach specific goals — buying a house, financing college education, and retiring (both early and late) — the real goal is to amass wealth.

WORKING ASSUMPTIONS

Because none of us knows the future, we're going to make assumptions about rates of return as we build these portfolios. That's okay for several reasons. First, we're looking at rather long time periods in which it is likely that returns will tend to average out about where they've been over the past seventy years. Second, we're going to use conservative assumptions, both to offer you some cushion in case returns fall below historical averages for a prolonged period of time and to factor in the costs, mostly fees and taxes, that your investments carry (but which the commonly used indexes by which the markets are measured don't incur). For example, the historical compound average annual return for large U.S. stocks, represented by Standard & Poor's 500 stock index, is 11.3 percent, and the return for small U.S. stocks is an even more robust 12.6 percent. But for our purposes we'll use a 10 percent average annual return and assume your stock holdings are spread in some ratio among big, medium, and small stocks. Bonds are a little trickier because historical calculations provide an average annual total return, which captures both the yield and the capital gain or loss on bonds. But since we intend not to trade bonds, but to hold them to maturity, the capital component isn't particularly relevant. What's more, since we're using inflation-indexed bonds, which are only a few years old, there isn't sufficient history to judge their capital performance. Because of that inflation protection, which will boost the yield if inflation rises, we're assuming a portfolio of inflation-indexed bonds will yield 6 percent annually. If it works out lower in reality, that's okay because inflation will have been modest. If inflation rises sharply, the bonds will offer some protection.

But be forewarned: Whether stocks have an average annual return of 12.6 percent, 11.3 percent, or 10 percent doesn't mean they will perform that way every year. In fact, I can guarantee you they won't. There will be spectacular years of gains, as there were in the last half of the 1990s, when returns averaged in excess of 20 percent annually, marking the best five-year period in the history of U.S. stocks. But there will also be years of crushing losses. And in between the extremes will be boring years of just above and just below average returns. Your challenge is to be constantly aware that you are investing for the long term and not to be spooked into running from your portfolio in the bad times or becoming euphoric and selling your house to invest in stocks in the good times. Steady as she goes, as the ship captain says.

PROFIT AND PAIN: WORST-CASE SCENARIOS

That's easier said than done, however. One of the things that will become very obvious as you examine these portfolios is that the all-stock portfolios have the best long-term results. Thus the temptation for many of us will be to say, "That's the one for me," and go about building an all-stock portfolio while blithely ignoring the fact that stocks are volatile. Sometimes they're very volatile. So before we go any further, let's look at some "worst-case" scenarios. What you'll see in front of you are just raw numbers that on the page look very sterile. I'm going to ask you to use your imagination as you look at those numbers to put some emotional content in them. Only you know what those emotions are and how well the fear and anxiety that any normal person will experience in the face of a financial cataclysm can be offset by rational thinking, planning, and adjustment.

It should already be obvious—and I'll make it even more obvious in this chapter—that time is an investor's best friend. A twenty-five-year-old investor will usually be better equipped to deal with a steep decline in stock prices than a fifty-five-year-old investor for two simple reasons. First, the twenty-five-year-old probably won't have much at stake, while the fifty-five-year-old investor may be doing frequent calculations of portfolio values to determine if she can retire at age sixty. To the twenty-five-year-old a 25 percent decline in a $35,000 portfolio represents a paper loss of $8,750, about the price of an older used car. To the fifty-five-year-old investor who has diligently built a portfolio worth $2 million, that same 25 percent decline represents a loss of _half a million dol-_

lars, the equivalent of perhaps three years' salary or six years of comfortable retirement living. But more important, the twenty-five-year-old investor has a potential forty years or more to recover from his loss and a career that is in its earliest stages, with promotions, raises, and offers from competing employers in the years ahead. The fifty-five-year-old investor's career probably has reached a plateau, no offers are coming from competing employers, and her health may not be the best. It's hard to be optimistic in the face of losing a quarter of the value of a portfolio built up over a lifetime under those circumstances.

Since the stock market collapse of 1929 that ushered in the Great Depression, there have been twenty years in which stocks declined in price. The average loss in those years was 12.3 percent, a decline that many market pros, in their efforts to minimize the psychological effect of falling prices, call a "correction." To those who came to investing in the roaring bull market of the 1990s, even a one-year loss seems like a disaster. But in the overall scheme of things a loss of that magnitude isn't a big deal. After all, the average annual return on large stocks is only a little less than that, and the return on small stocks is more than 12.3 percent. The pain really begins when the drops are more precipitous and longer lasting. Imagine having much of your personal wealth tied to the stock market in 1930. From 1930 through 1932 stock prices sustained a loss of 61 percent. The loss itself was bad enough, but the fact that it occurred over a three-year period turned it from shocking to fearsomely relentless.

How would our twenty-five-year-old budding investor with a $35,000 portfolio react today as he watched it shrink to just $13,650? There's a good chance he would never come back to the stock market. And our poor fifty-five-year-old looking forward to retirement with her $2 million portfolio would see it crushed to just $780,000, a loss of $1.2 million, the equivalent of twelve years' salary or twenty-four years of retirement living. Of course, you say, that was years ago. It can't happen again. But it can. It certainly isn't likely, but one lesson the markets teach constantly is that investors should never say "never." A much more recent, albeit less horrific, decline occurred in 1973 and 1974, when stocks fell 37 percent. If that happened today, our twenty-five-year-old investor would lose $12,950 on his $35,000 portfolio and the fifty-five-year-old would-be retiree would see her portfolio fall by $740,000.

Now consider what would have happened in that 1930–1932 period if our investors had been holding various percentages of their portfolios in bonds, which would have continued paying their stated interest rate regardless of what happened to the prices of stocks. With a $35,000 portfolio that held 60 percent stocks ($21,000) and 40 percent bonds ($14,000), our young investor would see a total decline in his stock portfolio of $12,810, while we assume his bonds would remain worth $14,000. So his overall loss of $12,810 would amount to just 37 percent. That's bad enough, but it's just over half the loss he would have experienced in an all-stock portfolio (in the period of 1930–1933 bond prices actually rose, giving a 60/40 portfolio a decline of just 30 percent; but since we're buying and holding bonds with no intention of selling them, that's a moot point). And if our fifty-five-year-old friend had $1.2 million in stocks and $800,000 in bonds, she would have suffered a loss of $732,000 rather than $1.2 million (the loss would have been even less—$604,000—if we'd counted the rise in bond prices). And a 40 percent stocks/60 percent bonds portfolio would have lost just $8,540 for the young investor and $488,000 for our older investor.

I've dealt here only with how stock market volatility can produce horrifying losses. It's also capable of producing stunning gains. It's the losses you need to be concerned about, because they are what will challenge you most in your efforts to stick to a long-term plan. After all, no one is going to complain if stocks produce a *gain* of 60 percent in any given year. But before the frightening results I just cited convince you to abandon all thoughts of a stock portfolio, remember that time *really is* your friend. While stocks are very volatile in the short run, that volatility eases considerably as time passes. The past performance of the stock market indicates that the level of volatility measured statistically declines by half in just five years and by half again in another five years. Thus the long-term investor with a ten-year or longer time horizon has little to fear as long as he or she can stomach the occasional sudden lurch down while also giving up assumptions that stocks will produce huge sustained gains. In many of the hypothetical portfolios that follow, I show the results for all-stock portfolios. I do that to give you an idea of what is possible at the higher average returns that are characteristic of stocks. But be very careful when applying those returns to your own situation. You have to assume that in the real world there will be years of losses that you will have to find some way to weather. If you do choose to go with all-stock portfolios, give yourself some wiggle room. You can do that by using even lower estimated rates of return than the already conservative figures we're using or by setting targets in excess of what you probably will need. I'm totally in favor of all-stock portfolios as the best way to increase your net worth, but there's no doubt you'll have to find a way to cope with volatility.

REBALANCING

Here's one last concept that you should know about as you lay the groundwork for your lifetime investment portfolio: rebalancing. At some point you'll come up with an optimum balance between stocks and bonds in your portfolio (and types of stocks within that stock portion, such as small-cap, large-cap, and foreign) with which you're comfortable. You don't have to do it right away. In fact, I urge anyone under age thirty-five to concentrate 100 percent of a portfolio in stocks. But as you grow older, as your portfolio increases in value, and as you near financial milestones in your life, a properly balanced portfolio will become more important. The trouble is that portfolios don't remain balanced. Let's say you choose an optimum portfolio mix of 60 percent stocks and 40 percent bonds, which is sort of the financial industry standard for a mature investor. Over time the stock portion of the portfolio will grow faster than the bond portion and will, at some point, amount to 70 percent or 80 percent of the value, all without your doing anything. If you're not paying attention, you will have a portfolio that is riskier than what you thought you wanted. To avoid that, you need to "rebalance" your portfolio periodically to restore it to the 60/40 ratio you determined you wanted in the first place. While you could sell some of your stock holdings and use the proceeds to buy more bonds, that involves taking profits and being taxed on them. A better way is to skew the amount of new money you're contributing to the portfolio toward bonds and away from stocks. If you pay a little attention to your portfolio, you can finetune it by adjusting the amounts going to stocks and bonds once or twice a year before it ever gets out of whack. And as you get closer and closer to retirement and think you want even more stability, you can gradually increase the bond ratio even though the stock portion is growing faster from simple price appreciation.

I've tried to create conditions for each portfolio that are fairly typical of people at certain ages and with certain incomes, but obviously everyone's situation is different, at least to some degree. You may be able to invest more or less than the amounts in the hypothetical portfolios. Use them only as a general guide, not as marching orders from which you can never deviate. Investing is a lifelong process, and as you learn more from experience you'll become more confident in charting your own financial course. And that is what financial freedom truly is all about.

6

GETTING AN EARLY START:
Portfolios for Long Time Horizons
(and Little Money)

IF SOMEONE TWENTY-FIVE YEARS OLD is really interested in investing, that interest is probably focused on day trading or hot tech stocks. Retirement is decades away, and concepts such as "buy and hold" and index funds aren't something you talk about on the ski slopes or at the beach. For many people in this age bracket, expenses are high—clothes, cars, entertainment, and rent—and incomes, while rising, aren't at levels that suggest real wealth is right around the corner. Yet this is the exact best time to set up a core investment program, even on a small scale. Relatively puny amounts of money today can, through compounding over many years, grow to become amazing amounts. And it all takes so little time and effort that it won't make a dent in career and social activities. The name of the game at this stage is stocks and only stocks, although this is also a time to be building savings in a money market account as well if you think you may be interested in making a down payment on a house or condominium in the next several years.

We have to start somewhere, so let's begin with a single person working for a medium-size company in a medium-size city. We'll assume that between casual efforts to tuck away a little salary in the company's credit union and a gift from parents, you have $5,000 that isn't in immediate danger of being spent. We'll also assume that you've just become eligible to participate in your company's 401(k) plan. What steps should you take?

Keeping in mind that investment portfolios take time to create and mold into shape, we'll set up a five-year plan for you. That's about the right time horizon to expect that some kind of big financial change will affect you—marriage, another job, a move to another city—that will require rethinking and adjusting your investment plans.

The first step is obvious: Jump into that 401(k) plan head-first. Not only will that be an important part of retirement plans decades from now, but, more practically, it's a way to get *free money!* Since funds that an employee contributes to a 401(k) aren't taxed in the year they're contributed, the federal government is, in effect, giving you money, which is reason enough to make the maximum contribution allowed. And since your employer probably contributes something to match your contributions, that's a second dose of free money you wouldn't otherwise have.

Where to put it? Stocks, stocks, and more stocks. Study the investment options offered under the plan and select mutual funds that invest entirely in stocks. If your plan offers a wide array of choices, diversify by choosing separate funds that invest in big stocks, small stocks, and international stocks. But if only one stock fund is available, take it. Don't bother with bond funds or money market funds or even balanced funds. They aren't where the money is over the long haul. And be especially careful about picking your own company's stock if it is offered as part of the plan. You've already got one of your most valuable possessions—your career—invested there, and you need the diversity offered by mutual funds.

Now that you're maxed out at the office, it's time to set up your own investment portfolio with that $5,000 you have tucked away. First, assume you'll keep $2,000 to meet possible emergencies, including the cost of moving to that new city or to cover living expenses if the worst should happen and you lose your job. So now you're down to $3,000 to start your portfolio. We'll assume, too, that you're paying more attention to your personal finances and will be able to invest another $2,400 a year to feed to your new portfolio. Of course, more is better if you can fit additional savings and investments into your lifestyle. The danger is that if you strain too hard to save now and deny yourself too many pleasures, you'll become discouraged and give up on the whole process. In the end, that would be the biggest mistake of all.

At this point you have two choices: simplicity or flexibility. You can set up a simple portfolio that will last you a lifetime with only two mutual funds. One will reflect the performance of the entire U.S. stock market, from giant companies like Microsoft down to little companies you've never heard of. The other will reflect the performance of much of the rest of the world, including stock markets in *countries* you might never have heard of. The advantage of this approach, of course, is that little decision making or monitoring is required. A once-a-year check to rebalance may be all you need to do. The disadvantage is that such a portfolio is pretty boring, sort of like riding a train all night: nothing to do, nothing much to see.

The alternative is to make up a more flexible portfolio with index funds that represent different sectors of both the U.S. and foreign markets. Typically you would start with an S&P 500 index fund, which contains many of the largest and most powerful companies in the world, including a healthy dose of big technology companies. That would be supplemented by another index fund that represents a cross section of small U.S. companies (some of which will grow to become giants a decade or two from now, others of which will quietly go bankrupt or be bought out) and by a third · fund that represents companies deemed midcap, or medium-size. How you combine the percentages of those three funds will determine to some extent the volatility and long-term returns of your portfolio. Historically, small stocks have been more volatile than large stocks, but they've also afforded slightly better returns (11.3 percent for large stocks, 12.6 percent for small stocks). If you want to take that risk, you can simply tilt your new investments more toward the small-cap fund than the large-cap fund to yield a blended portfolio that is weighted more heavily toward small-caps than the single all-encompassing domestic fund in our simple portfolio. You still want a little international exposure and can even break that up into market segments, such as European, Asian, and emerging markets funds. Besides being able to tilt toward riskier, more rewarding market segments, a flexible fund is inherently more interesting to build than a simple portfolio, provided you accept the additional risks. A single broad U.S. index fund won't fall as far or rise as high as any one of the market segment funds in the flexible portfolio. But if the idea of a 25 percent or 30 percent decline in one fund is enough to scare you into selling one of the funds in your flexible portfolio, *don't go there*. And keep in mind that most people can intellectually accept the idea of such a loss, but when it happens they still panic and run. As we'll see now, it takes longer to set up a flexible portfolio if you don't have enough money on hand to buy the minimum amounts that fund companies require of new investors.

THE SIMPLE PORTFOLIO

Here's how to build, in stages, the simple portfolio consisting of a total market U.S. index fund and a broad-based international index fund. Because you have to invest a certain minimum to buy any fund, the portfolio will be a little heavy in international stocks in the early stages. But by skewing your additional investments more heavily toward the U.S. fund in subsequent years, you'll reach the right balance of about 75 percent domestic and 25 percent international in five years. The plan is to start with a total U.S. domestic fund. A year later, after you've accumulated another $2,400 in savings, buy the international index fund. During the course of that year your domestic fund will have earned, on average, about 10 percent, or $300. In the third year your domestic fund earns another 10 percent on the $3,300 now in it, and your international fund earns $240. That's when you begin regular investments in each fund. By putting $2,000 of your $2,400 in annual savings in the domestic fund and $400 in the international fund, you begin moving the balance of the two toward the 75 percent/25 percent ratio that's probably optimum for most investors. "The Simple Portfolio" table shows the results year by year.

THE SIMPLE PORTFOLIO

	U.S. Mkt. Index	Foreign Index	Total	Percentages
Beginning of:				
Year 1	$ 3,000	—	$ 3,000	100% dom./0% foreign
Year 2	$ 3,300	$2,400	$ 5,700	58% dom./42% foreign
Year 3	$ 5,630	$3,040	$ 8,670	65% dom./35% foreign
Year 4	$ 8,193	$3,744	$11,937	69% dom./31% foreign
Year 5	$11,012	$4,518	$15,530	71% dom./29% foreign

There you have it: a simple portfolio that, tended to occasionally and added to annually (hopefully with increasing amounts of savings being added), will yield huge amounts of money later in life.

THE FLEXIBLE PORTFOLIO

Simple may be boring, so we can also consider constructing a more flexible portfolio. The flexible portfolio is, like the simple portfolio, accomplished in stages. The difference is that there are more stages, so it takes a little longer to erect the structure. But after that you can simply add new money to each component of the portfolio in varying amounts to achieve the plan you want. We'll start with $3,000 in the "core of the core," an S&P 500 index fund. A year later, with the $2,400 you've been able to save, buy a small-cap index fund, preferably one that tracks the Russell 2000 index of small-cap stocks. Another year later, another $2,400 goes to a midcap index fund. A final $2,400 a year later buys an international index fund. At the end of the fourth year, then, you will have a portfolio worth $13,130, allocated as follows:

S&P 500 index fund: $4,392 (33%)
Small-cap index fund: $3,194 (24%)
Midcap index fund: $2,904 (22%)
International index fund: $2,640 (20%)
(Does not add to 100% due to rounding.)

That's a very nice distribution across various market segments. Of course, these portfolios are theoretical. In the course of five years the prices of the funds you buy early in the program won't have moved exactly 10 percent per year, so your distribution across the four funds and the return you earn will doubtless be somewhat different. Whatever it is, you can bring it into the shape you want in the fifth year by distributing your $2,400 in new savings among the four funds in different proportions. The natural inclination is to put new money into the fund or funds that have performed the best. The true long-term investors' decision, however, will be to put it in the fund or funds that have performed the worst. After all, that's where the cheap stocks are.

If you do the math, you'll notice that the simple portfolio at the end of the fifth year is worth $17,082, while the flexible portfolio is worth $16,832. That small difference is due to the compounding effect of the same new investments in just two funds rather than across four. But again, these are hypothetical portfolios; the real world won't be nearly so neat.

One thing I want to make very clear: These are all just suggested portfolios. As you gain knowledge and experience in investing, you should think about tailoring your portfolio to suit your own needs and financial situation. Here are some examples—I call them variations on the theme—of ways in which you might tailor the portfolios we've already discussed to suit your own circumstances.

STAY AT HOME

I like the diversifying effects of foreign stocks, and so do many professional financial advisers. But are they necessary to a well-balanced and successful long-term portfolio? Not at all. So if you're uncomfortable having some of your money sitting in places like Brazil, Thailand, Japan, or Italy, you should opt for comfort and simply discard the international funds from these recommended portfolios. That, of course, leaves you with the ultimate in simple portfolios—just one fund. And in your flexible portfolio you're spreading your savings over three funds instead of four, so it takes a year less to set up the portfolio.

CONSERVATIVE BEYOND YOUR YEARS

So you think having your investment portfolio invested 100 percent in stocks is taking a little too much risk? That's fine, you can temper it. In both the simple and the flexible portfolios all you need to do is allocate $1,000 in each year to buying a ten-year, inflation-indexed bond at the Treasury's regular auction, cutting back on contributions to the total market fund or to the various market segment funds proportionately. You'll have to pay income taxes on the interest the bonds pay, but you're probably not in the highest income tax brackets yet. (I hear people complaining about being in the top bracket all the time. What's the beef? That means your income is up there among the elite, so quit whining.) And if you find this conservative posture is comfortable, simply keep replacing each maturing rung of your bond ladder with a fatter rung—say, $2,000 or $2,500. By the time you're ready for retirement you'll have a very healthy income stream from your bond holdings, and bonds will be maturing annually in case you need access to even more money. But if you change your mind and find stocks more appealing as you go through your financial life, it isn't hard to divert new money from bonds to stocks.

CORE AND EXPLORE PORTFOLIOS

You know the stats: 75 percent of professional money managers fail to beat the market. Still, you want to give it a shot. Fair enough. Better to do it now, when you can afford to lose some ground, than later, when it will be harder to recover from losses. Set up your S&P 500 fund with $3,000, then start a "shadow" portfolio of stocks you think would make good buys. Just don't buy them yet. Wait until you have that full $2,400 saved, then buy however many shares you can of a single company (you have the diversity of the S&P 500 fund to protect you). Be sure to keep records of your trading costs. When you have another $2,400 saved, it goes to the index fund. The next $2,400 goes to another favored stock, and the final $2,400 goes to the index fund. It's up to you when to decide to take your profits (or your losses) on the individual stocks. Keep a running tally on how the stocks are performing against the S&P, and don't cheat by forgetting to include things like trading commissions and taxes. If you do well and have some fun with individual stocks, you can continue to grow that portion of your portfolio over the years. But you'll have to buy another book for advice on playing that game. Just remember to keep a total market or S&P 500 index fund at the core of your portfolio, using individual stocks to "flavor" the portfolio.

POOLED RESOURCES

Married or just living together, it's a fact that two should be able to live more cheaply together than apart. Where there were two rents, now there is one. Just send that excess monthly rent check to a mutual fund instead of a landlord and you'll be on the way to laying the foundation of a very lucrative long-term investment program. And it's important for a couple to take this step now, while there's excess cash flow. Later on, expenses like down payments on houses and bills for things like furniture and carpets (and maybe strollers and nannies) begin to enter the picture. To illustrate my point, let's look at two couples who take very different approaches to this period in their lives. Jason and Janet strive to save and invest as much as they can before they start a family because Janet is ambivalent about working when the kids are young. When Janet quits working at age thirty-two, they'll have $45,000 invested in a portfolio of stocks. But Steve and Joy figure they'll take full advantage of their two incomes to sample every restaurant within fifty miles and to take some really fantastic trips before settling down to have kids at age thirty-two. As a consequence they delay starting any investment program until they're in their early forties. It takes them five years of saving $10,000 a year to put a total of $50,000 to work in their investment portfolio. Both portfolios provide 10 percent annual returns. In the table titled "It's Never Too Early to Start Investing" we see what subsequent years look like financially if nothing else changes.

IT'S NEVER TOO EARLY TO START INVESTING

	Jason/Janet Portfolio	Steve/Joy Portfolio
Age 32	$ 45,000	$ 0
Age 40	$ 96,451	$ 0
Age 42	$ 116,718	$ 10,000
Age 43	$ 128,390	$ 21,000
Age 44	$ 141,229	$ 33,100
Age 45	$ 155,352	$ 46,410
Age 46	$ 170,887	$ 61,051
Age 47	$ 187,976	$ 67,156
Age 50	$ 250,196	$ 89,385
Age 60	$ 648,944	$231,841
Age 65	$1,045,131	$373,382

Without saving or investing another dime after Janet quits working to have children, she and Jason will be millionaires when it comes time to retire, while Steve and Joy face an uncertain retirement a best. It's all the result of letting compounding work over a longer period of time. It's never too early to start investing!

Now let's get back to the portfolio construction that couples in their late twenties might want to undertake. The simple and flexible portfolios that we built for the single men and women in this section are useful models for anyone this age. The only difference is the amounts that might flow into them. And the picture is a little complicated by decisions about how to save for coming expenses, principally a down payment on a house or condo and the arrival of children, if that's in the plans. A single person intending to become half of a couple at some future date might have these same concerns but will have fewer resources to work with and probably less certainty about when the expenses might occur.

The options in saving for a house down payment range anywhere between extremes: certainty and risk. The certain approach dictates that a couple decide early on how much house they want to take on and begin laying aside the necessary money in a money market account to reach their goal when they need the money. The risky approach is to forgo the savings account and put that money in the stock market. If the market is good to you, you'll either reach your goal earlier or you'll have a bigger down payment when the original target date finally arrives. A blended approach calls for some amount to be saved in a stable money market account while other money is put at risk in the market. Remember that the interest from the money market account is constantly being taxed at ordinary income tax rates, while the money accumulating in a stock fund isn't taxed unless and until you remove it at profitable prices, and even then it's taxed at the lower capital gains rate. Let's look at two portfolios that illustrate the possibilities inherent in the extreme approaches to amassing a $50,000 down payment over five years.

First, we'll assume you will put $10,000 into a money market account each year for five years, that the money market account yields 4 percent annually, and that you're in the 28 percent tax bracket. The table titled "The Money Market Account" shows the results. Then we'll look at that same investment put into a stock fund that has an average annual yield of 10 percent, and we'll look at it two ways. First, we'll see what a smooth gain of 10 percent a year for all five years produces (see table titled "The Smooth Stock Market Account"). Then we'll see what happens if you have a smooth gain of 10 percent in the first four years followed by a 20 percent decline in the fifth year.

THE MONEY MARKET ACCOUNT

Beginning of year 1: $10,000 invested
End of year 1: After-tax value: $10,288

Beginning of year 2: $10,288 plus additional $10,000 = $20,288
End of year 2: After-tax value: $20,873

Beginning of year 3: $20,873 plus additional $10,000 = $30,873
End of year 3: After-tax value: $31,762

Beginning of year 4: $31,762 plus additional $10,000 = $41,762
End of year 4: After-tax value: $42,964

Beginning of year 5: $42,964 plus additional $10,000 = $52,964
End of year 5: After-tax value: $54,490

Now we'll do the same portfolio assuming a smooth 10 percent annual gain from stocks, which aren't taxed unless and until you sell them at a profit. Shares held longer than one year get the favorable long-term capital gains tax rate, while shares held less than a year pay taxes at the equivalent of ordinary income tax rates.

THE SMOOTH STOCK MARKET ACCOUNT

Beginning of year 1: $10,000
Value at end of year 1: $11,000

Beginning of year 2: $11,000 plus additional $10,000 = $21,000
Value at end of year 2: $23,100

Beginning of year 3: $23,100 plus additional $10,000 = $33,100
Value at end of year 3: $36,410

Beginning of year 4: $36,410 plus additional $10,000 = $46,410
Value at end of year 4: $51,051

Beginning of year 5: $51,051 plus additional $10,000 = $61,051
Value at end of year 5: $67,156

To liquidate account for house down payment:
Pay 14% long-term capital gains on $11,051 in capital gains during first four years and 28% short-term capital gains on $6,105 earned in final year
Total tax bill: $3,256
Available funds for down payment: $63,900

Quite a difference, isn't there, between the returns and onerous taxes on the money market account and the returns and more kindly tax treatment of the stock market account? But that's the price of certainty. And certainty can be a very nice thing, as we see now when we examine what happens when a typical bear market (defined as a drop in stock prices of 20 percent or more) hits just before you're ready to make that down payment on the house.

Nothing changes in the first four years of the account. But just after the beginning of the fifth year (just after you have sunk that final $10,000 chunk of savings into the market), stocks nosedive 20 percent and stay down for the remainder of the year. While you started the fifth year with $61,051, suddenly you have just $48,841—not even enough to make the down payment. And you still owe long-term capital gains taxes on some of your early purchases, which remain profitable despite the market's big decline.

DEDICATED DINKs (DUAL-INCOME, NO KIDS)

While kids and home ownership have long been part of the fabled American dream, not everyone opts to have children or to own a home. And some couples decide early on that neither is in the cards for them. From a financial point of view, that decision opens the door to lots of possibilities, including the prospect of a very comfortable early retirement, interruptions in careers for adventure, or simply the amassing of a great deal of wealth. Remember Jason and Janet, who saved $45,000 before starting a family—and how their plan contrasted with that of Steve and Joy, who chose to wait until their forties to begin a serious investment program? Recall that at age fifty Jason and Janet had a portfolio valued at about $250,000 and had a million dollars in assets at age sixty-five. Steve and Joy, who started investing $10,000 a year in their early forties, had only about $90,000 at age fifty and were looking at the prospect of retiring at age sixty-five with just $375,000 in their portfolio. Let's take a look now at another couple, Bill and Carol, who chose not to have kids. They began investing $10,000 a year in a portfolio that returned an average 10 percent each year, and they kept investing that amount through thick and thin. How their portfolios look at different ages is shown in the table "Steady as She Goes."

STEADY AS SHE GOES

	Portfolio Value
Age 32	$ 10,000
Age 35	$ 49,720
Age 40	$ 147,231
Age 50	$ 557,190
Age 53	$1,190,165

There it is: after making relatively modest annual investments in a stock portfolio, Bill and Carol can, if they choose, retire at age fifty-three with a million dollars. Had they started investing earlier than age thirty-two, they would have been millionaires that much sooner. And if they choose not to retire, but go on working and investing, it will be less than seven years before that million-dollar nest egg has doubled to become more than $2 million.

This certainly isn't intended as an argument against children and houses. It merely illustrates the possibilities that exist. Either of the other two couples, had they chosen to somehow find $10,000 a year to invest, even if the wife and mother wasn't working, could be in the same position or better at age fifty-three.

7

GETTING SERIOUS:

Portfolios for Your Thirties

MANY PEOPLE BEGIN TO GET SERIOUSLY INTERESTED in investing in their mid-thirties. College for their kids may still be several years away, but they're beginning to hear horror stories from parents of older children about the huge financial drain tuition can be. Many own a home, have become comfortable with the mortgage payments, and have realized just how lucrative those mortgage interest tax deductions can be. Careers are blossoming and incomes are rising, including bonuses and perhaps grants of stock options. If they have been smart enough to take full advantage of their employers' 401(k) plans, they're beginning to see serious amounts of money in their accounts.

All things considered, it's a good thing people get interested at this age. They still have time to amass a considerable fortune for their retirements, and they can lay out reasonable plans to meet college expenses that may still be a decade away. For couples without kids, the first inklings of early retirement possibilities begin to surface, and we'll examine early retirement as a goal in this section. For those who don't grasp the importance of saving and investment at this age, things are going to get progressively more difficult as time passes. But we'll deal with that later.

SINGLES AND DINKs IN THEIR THIRTIES

We'll start this discussion of early middle age (that's right—you're no longer considered to be really "young," even though you probably feel that you still are) with DINKs and singles, since they have the most flexibility in what they can do with their money. But first, take this short test on personal finance:

I am contributing the maximum amount to my 401(k) plan: T or F

At least 80 percent or more of my 401(k) portfolio is in stocks: T or F

I do not incur any interest charges on my credit cards: T or F

If you answered "true" to all three questions, congratulations: you're a financial adult. If you answered "false" to any one of the three questions, you've got to get your financial act together. The benefits of tax-advantaged investing are too great and the drain of carrying needless debt too large to tolerate anything less than a 100 percent passing score. Take whatever steps are necessary to make sure three months from now that you can pass this little quiz with flying colors.

For single people and couples who intend to remain childless, the basic portfolio that we laid out for twenty-somethings (see page 145) will work just fine as a starting point for building a long-term investment plan. It can be the same simple one- or two-fund portfolio consisting of a total U.S. stock market index fund combined with a broad-based international index fund. If you don't like the foreign exposure, scrap the international fund and invest everything in the U.S. index fund. Or the portfolio can offer a little more flexibility by being divided in various ratios among a variety of index funds: large-cap, midcap, and small-cap U.S. funds and even those representing various segments of international markets, such as emerging markets or those in Asia or Europe. These all-stock portfolios are well suited to be the foundation of a simple, lifelong approach to investing that, coupled with fully funded retirement plans, will produce astounding returns. Once this portfolio has been up and running a while, you will find that you can reduce the amounts you hold in money market funds or in bonds. If you need a new car or want to take a two-week jaunt to Europe, you'll usually be better off pulling money out of your stock fund portfolio, with its low capital gains taxes, than saving for the car or trip in a money market account with its lower average returns and regular income tax treatment of interest payments. Certainly you won't have to finance either the car or the vacation with borrowed money.

ESCAPING THE RAT RACE

This isn't an age when people typically think about retiring. Indeed, for most people with children, retiring significantly early simply isn't in the financial cards. But if you're thirty-five and single or married without kids, you can at least think about retiring as early as age fifty—or, if not retiring, then doing something different with your life. You have fifteen years to get your finances in shape, and as we'll see, it won't be easy. But it is possible. The trouble is, most people at this age aren't thinking that far ahead and fail to lay the financial groundwork now that will give them options later. The following exercise, aimed at producing a portfolio that will support retirement at age fifty, is worth examining even if you don't plan to retire early, because it demonstrates the complexities of retirement planning in an extreme situation. No matter when you retire, you'll face some of the same hurdles, although they will probably be considerably lower than those confronting early retirees.

You know very well that time is the friend of the long-term investor. But it's the sworn enemy of the early retiree. The problem is twofold: you have less time to amass an investment portfolio, *and* it has to last you much longer. Life expectancies for thirty-five-year-old Americans are around eighty these days. Retire at fifty and you must plan to cover thirty years, while your colleagues who work to age sixty-five typically need insure only about fifteen years of living expenses with a much larger retirement fund. That's also fifteen years more in which inflation can take its insidious toll, years in which you won't have an income to replenish the money lost to inflation's effects. Further complicating the planning for early retirement is that you usually can't touch your retirement plan assets until you're nearly sixty. So you're going to have to live off your money held outside retirement plans for ten years.

All this sounds daunting, and it is. But it is possible to escape the rat race early provided you're willing to start planning early, to make some sacrifices now to add substantially to savings, and to live a relatively frugal life once retired. And, of course, the beauty of planning for early retirement is that you don't have to go at age fifty. If you fall short of your retirement funding goals, just keep working and retire later—say at age fifty-two, fifty-five, or fifty-eight. For every additional year you work, you will have added more money to your portfolio and it will have to last you one year less.

Before we look at the actual numbers, here are the things you must plan for:

1. Having enough money to get you through the period before you can tap your formal retirement plans.
2. Having enough money both in retirement accounts and outside those accounts to provide a reasonable standard of living for thirty years while enduring some estimated rate of inflation.
3. Deciding if you will live only off the returns from your capital or if you will gradually eat away at the capital to fund living expenses.
4. Deciding whether in retirement you want certain income from bonds, with their lower returns, or will risk the volatility of stocks to get the higher average returns.

The easiest way to approach early retirement planning is to work backward from a target. The target is based on your estimate of what you want to live on stated in today's dollars, then projected out forty-five years at some estimated rate of inflation. Let's say you think carefully about where and how you would live in retirement right now if you had that option, and you determined that you could do very nicely on $90,000 a year. That's $90,000 in _today's_ dollars. You have to determine how much that will be in inflation-adjusted dollars forty-five years from now. With inflation calculated to run an average of 4 percent per year, you'll need $162,000 in annual income at age fifty just to equal today's standard of living. Ten years later, when you become eligible to tap your 401(k) without penalty, you'll need $240,300 in annual income. And by the time you statistically die at age eighty, your living costs will have swelled to $526,257 per year. If inflation runs higher, the need for funds will rise as well.

How much money you need to reach that goal depends on your willingness to take risks. The loftiest target—the no-risk approach—is to have enough money that you can own a portfolio of bonds that, coupled with Social Security payments, will throw off the full amount you would need at the end of your life. That way you need never touch your capital. Less certain, but much more attainable, is a plan that calls for you to eat into your capital while receiving a steadily decreasing stream of earnings from bonds, supplemented, of course, by Social Security. The goal: to die nearly broke. Those same two approaches can be taken with a stock portfolio, the caveat being the uncertainty of precise returns in any given year. Remember that your stock portfolio is aimed at lasting forty-five years, which is plenty of time to assume you would earn the average 10 percent per year that we're assuming stocks will produce. It's just that some years will be better—much better—than others, and there will be some very lean years in which stock returns are negative.

The resources you will have to achieve those sums of money will depend a lot on your efforts to save and invest over the next fifteen years. Even though you can't touch your retirement funds until age 59½, your combined retirement plans will be the major supply of funds for retirement. You'll be contributing to the plans for another fifteen years, and the portfolios will then continue to compound for an additional ten years after that before you begin to tap them. So let's look at what we might reasonably expect from retirement plans in the table "A Working Couple's Approach to Early Retirement." It should go without saying that anyone trying to retire early will be entirely invested in stocks. If you want an all-bond portfolio to produce predictable income in retirement, you would switch from stocks to bonds near the time of retirement.

A WORKING COUPLE'S APPROACH TO EARLY RETIREMENT

Balance in 401(k) at age 35	$ 120,000
Annual additions (total of both workers)	$ 15,200
Value at age 50 retirement	$1,025,516
Value at age 60 (10 years of compounding only)	$2,666,342
Income at 6% (bond yield)	$ 159,980
Income at 10% (average stock returns)	$ 266,634
Income needed to keep up with 4% inflation:	
At age 60	$ 240,300
At age 65	$ 293,166
At age 80	$ 526,257

As you can see, a bond portfolio won't begin to cover your living expenses when you start tapping your 401(k), while a stock portfolio will. Stocks even provide a substantial cushion that will enable you to make ends meet in years in which the market is flat or down. But even the stock portfolio falls woefully short of providing sufficient returns to carry you through your final fifteen years. If you don't have other assets to make up the difference, you will have to begin at some point eating into your principal. It should be obvious that between two investments, the one with the higher return either will last longer given the same size withdrawals or will permit higher withdrawals. An investment yielding 6 percent, for example, will last only eight years if you withdraw 15 percent of it annually, while that same amount invested to return 10 percent will last eleven years.

There are two ways to approach the depletion of capital: level income, which provides you with the same amount every year, or rising income, which provides less money at first than the level plan but more money later as inflation forces your costs of living higher. The difference is significant. Given the $2,666,000 in our early retiree's 401(k) plans at age sixty, here's what the various options look like:

Annual Withdrawals to Deplete $2,666,000 over Twenty Years

Level income bond portfolio (6%): $219,145
Level income stock portfolio (10%): $284,729
Rising income bond portfolio (6%): $158,893 first year,
    rising 4% annually, ending in the twentieth year with
    income of $347,976
Rising income stock portfolio (10%): $215,679 first year,
    rising 4% annually, ending in the twentieth year with
    income of $472,337

Either way you have a problem: While the level income approach with stocks provides ample money early on, it will fall far short in your later years. The rising income approach using stocks doesn't cover your cost of living at any point, but it doesn't fall nearly so far short in the later years as the level approach. Bonds come up short in both cases, but at least you have a degree of certainty about the actual amount coming to you in any given year.

Social Security will narrow the gap some—perhaps completely if you use the rising income stock portfolio and Social Security payments continue to be indexed for inflation. If inflation rises sharply, all bets are off. But if it averages less than 4 percent annually, the financial strain will ease.

The solution, then, is to have an investment portfolio outside of your retirement plans that will take you through ten years of early retirement and that will still have enough money to supplement your retirement funds. Remember that you calculated you would need $162,000 of income when you retire at age fifty and $240,300 the year you turn sixty and begin to withdraw money from your retirement plans. The question, then, is how much must you have when you retire at age fifty? The answer—$1.3 million—may seem impossible, but don't abandon your plans yet. Based on depletion calculations, if you had $1.3 million invested in stocks at age fifty, you could withdraw $165,000 annually and still have $300,000 left when you turn sixty. That $300,000, added to your IRA kitty of $2,666,000, gives you a total of $2,966,000 to cover ages sixty through eighty. That amount, using a stock portfolio and the rising income method of withdrawals, provides you with $240,000 of income at age sixty—right on target—and the annual increase of 4 percent each year until your portfolio is exhausted at age eighty.

I know, you're asking how in the world can you save $1.3 million in just fifteen years? Here's where compounding demonstrates its enormous powers yet again. If you and your partner can save $28,000 in the first year and can then increase that amount by 4 percent each year, you will have a total of $1,337,000 at the end of fifteen years. And that doesn't include any equity you might have in a house or other assets that you can liquidate to help fund your retirement. Now, $28,000 isn't small change for most of us, but a working couple that makes some sacrifices now at least has a shot at leaving the rat race plenty early enough to enjoy a long, although not lucrative, retirement. Good luck!

COUPLES WITH KIDS: THE TUITION TARGET

What about the rest of us, the soccer moms and dads who are looking at huge college bills just ten years away? How do we fund those? The choices, once again, range somewhere between the certainty of income from bonds and the higher, though volatile, returns of stocks. College educations are a little like retirement in that the expenses come over time. Not as much time, to be sure, but it's easy to imagine a family with two kids to educate who will be paying tuition bills for seven or eight years. So if your eldest kid is still ten years away from college, you could have eighteen years to see them both through graduation. That length of time is a powerful argument in favor of the higher returns of stocks as the core of a college education portfolio.

As with retirement, financing college educations is best done by working backward from a target. College costs have typically grown faster than the national inflation rate, although the torrid pace of a few years ago has slowed recently to about 4 percent annually (the national inflation rate has also slowed, to below 3 percent, although no one knows how long it will remain so well behaved), so we'll use 4 percent as our target rate. How much you'll pay depends, of course, on where the kids go to college. The College Board estimated that more than 70 percent of kids attending college in the 1998–99 school year had tuition costs of less than $8,000, and only about 6 percent paid more than $20,000 in tuition. Once room and board, texts, fees, and spending money are included, the costs of college today run between $7,000 and $25,000 a year. Since your kids are particularly smart and you want the best for them, we'll aim high and estimate today's college costs at $15,000. That means when your eldest kid starts college the first year will cost $22,200. When your youngest kid begins four years later, the cost will be $25,971, and when he or she graduates, that last year will have taken $29,214 out of your net worth. The total cost for eight years of college? A whopping $204,557.

The usual recommendation is for parents to invest in a mixture of stocks and bonds that eventually is shifted to bank accounts or money market accounts as the time to start paying for school draws nearer. That approach provides a degree of certainty that can be very comfortable if you are able to hit your goals or very uncomfortable if you come up short. The trouble with it is that it provides lower overall returns and you wind up paying a larger share of the college fund to the IRS through taxes on interest earnings than with an approach sticking mostly with stock funds. But using stock funds means you won't be as certain that you can meet each year's expenses. In the case of a shortfall from either the conventional approach to financing college or the all-stock approach, there are other sources of funds, including student loans, home equity loans, and a loan from your 401(k) plans.

Let's look at the two approaches with an eye toward meeting that $204,000 expense without using any borrowings. First, the traditional approach: We'll assume that a combined stock and bond fund will yield an average of about 8.5 percent for the ten years leading up to the first tuition payment and that it will then earn only nominal amounts as you exhaust it over an eight-year period. A program that has you investing $10,000 the first year and raising that amount 4 percent per year gets you to about $210,000 when your first kid starts college. Put that in a bank account and the beauty is that you know you have the costs of eight years of college covered. Indeed, you can turn your attention to putting the annual college contribution into your own retirement fund. The downside is that the college fund will be virtually depleted at the end of eight years.

A stock approach looks very different. First, let's assume you are able to contribute the same $10,000 the first year and keep increasing it 4 percent per year thereafter. At the higher returns available from stocks, you'll have a college fund worth $230,000 when your first kid starts college. As you take money out to pay for each year's college costs, the remainder continues to compound. The results are shown in the table "A Stock Market Approach to College."

A STOCK MARKET APPROACH TO COLLEGE
The First Year

Total college fund	$230,000
First year's costs	22,200
Balance	207,800
Earnings on balance	20,780
End of first-year fund	228,580
Net cost, first year	$ 1,420

The Last Year

Total college fund	$190,660
Eighth year's costs	29,214
Balance	161,446
Earnings on balance	16,145
End of eighth-year fund	177,591
Total net cost of college	$ 52,409

The results are impressive. Not only have you pared down the net cost of two very expensive college educations to something that most people can manage, you've also got a sizable chunk of money that can now be applied toward your long-term retirement goals. And we haven't even taken into account the annual college fund contribution that could be applied to your retirement portfolio during the eight years the kids are in college. Can something go wrong? Certainly. Over a period of eight years you would expect at least one year in which your market portfolio experiences a loss of some magnitude. That is why stocks are a riskier investment over the short term than bonds or money market and bank accounts. But given an eight-year horizon, chances are that the average returns of stocks would be about 10 percent, with good years offsetting poor years. And if you get worried about the years in which stocks produce subpar results, you can turn to home equity loans or a loan from your 401(k) to avoid further depleting the college fund.

Once again we're using two examples that occur at the extreme ends of a huge range of choices. The point is to illustrate that the conventional wisdom isn't necessarily the best when it comes to achieving financial goals.

8

TIME IS OF THE ESSENCE:
Portfolios for Your Forties

IF YOU'RE BECOMING SERIOUSLY INTERESTED in investing at this age, you're just in the nick of time. You're now squarely in the midst of middle age, and if you're like me, it's a bit startling how fast time is going by (here's a warning: It does nothing but accelerate from now on). Significant financial milestones are coming at you a lot faster than you would have thought or liked. If you have kids, for example, college probably isn't very far away, and you'll have to solve that problem soon (more on that shortly). Retirement is only fifteen to twenty years away. That doesn't give compounding much chance to work its magic on whatever you can save and invest. And, of course, there's much less time to recover from a financial disaster, either of a personal nature or, more broadly, the result of a sickly stock market.

The hurdles you must clear to do something about your financial situation are higher now than they would have been ten years ago, but they're certainly not insurmountable. A big obstacle that has kept many people from setting up a savings and investing program prior to this age is family. Rearing kids takes an enormous investment of time, energy, and money, so it isn't surprising that there hasn't been a lot of any of those left over for concentrating on long-term financial affairs. Other hurdles are purely psychological. Habits, for one thing, are probably tending to become deeply ingrained. Some of those habits—eating out often, buying new cars frequently, taking nice trips—may explain why you haven't taken much interest in savings and investing to this point. There just isn't enough money to do it all, so you have chosen to do those things you wanted to do at the moment. This isn't anything to be ashamed of, it's just reality. Now something is motivating you to change, for better or for worse. It's better if you (and your spouse, if you're married) have resolved to focus more on your finances than on the immediate gratification available from other ways of using your money. As you'll see, there are ways to get where you want to go by applying a little discipline to your financial lives. It's worse if you're panic-stricken about what to do about the kids' college tuition or your own retirements and you want to earn millions overnight. There are no reliable short-term solutions to increasing your wealth rapidly, and most people who attempt that feat wind up worse off than when they started.

Before deciding where you want to go, you need to figure out what's available to get you there. Simply put, you need to know two things: your net worth and your cash flow. Those two basic financial documents aren't hard to prepare and will give you a picture of what you have to work with to meet the pressing needs of tuition payments and to structure your finances to provide the maximum boost possible to your retirement plans. Start with net worth, since it's the easiest of the two to prepare. It's nothing more than the sum total of your assets and liabilities. Assets include money in the bank, funds held in 401(k) or other retirement accounts, and the value of your house and such significant possessions as cars and boats. Liabilities are the amounts you owe others, including mortgage debt, car loans, and credit card debt. There's a temptation in preparing this document to cheat a bit by assigning high values to such things as furniture and clothes. But the fact is that they're mostly worth what you could save on your tax bill by giving them to charities. Since you're the only who cares what your financial position is (unless you're applying for a mortgage), it doesn't make any sense to inflate the results.

What will you learn from preparing a net worth statement? In the broadest sense, it's a measure of your financial health. If the net worth statement is negative—you owe more than you have—you've got a serious problem that needs correction. You've been living beyond your means, and that's got to stop. Now. You might consider paying a fee-only financial consultant to review your finances to see what's causing the problem and to figure out ways to fix it. Positive net worth is good, and the more positive, the better.

But beyond that, you can also use your net worth statement to understand where your assets are and what you can do with them. If the bulk of your net worth is tied up in your house, you may want to think about refinancing it. By taking out a larger mortgage loan, you'll receive cash for some of that home equity that can then be put to work in the stock market, where returns are likely to be more lucrative. If you have money in your employer's 401(k) or other retirement account, perhaps it hasn't been invested as well as it could be. People who don't have time to learn a bit about investing usually opt for seemingly safe places—conservative investments with relatively low returns—for their retirement money, not realizing the opportunity for huge long-term gains that they're missing. In any event, preparing a net worth statement is a lot like having a physical when you aren't sick: it gives the doctor a benchmark to measure your health against in the coming years. By recalculating your net worth periodically—once a year is about right—you'll be able to measure your progress in taking control of your finances.

Not everything can be quantified and reduced to a line in a statement of net worth. This is the point where I'll introduce, as painlessly as I can, the subject of inheritance. Over the next twenty to forty years there will take place a truly massive transfer of wealth as the generation that created the modern American economy passes away. You who are in your mid-forties are doubtless already experiencing the pain of loss, whether it is in the form of the physical and mental deterioration of your parents and close relatives or in their actual death. Some families are more comfortable than others in discussing finances. If you have a reasonable idea of the amounts you can expect to inherit and how they are invested, that's additional information to take into account—not so much in drawing up your statement of net worth, but in making rough calculations about how you're going to achieve your own long-term financial goals. If, for example, your parents are highly conservative and have most of their assets in bonds or certificates of deposit, you can feel somewhat more comfortable devoting a larger portion of your own investment portfolio to stocks. If, on the other hand, your parents have investments in stocks, you might want to skew your own portfolio a tad more toward conservative investments. But never forget that circumstances change. Prolonged illness, the remarriage of a widowed parent, or any number of other unforeseen events can mean that you actually inherit considerably less than you expect. Plan accordingly.

A cash flow statement takes a little more time to prepare. If you skipped the first chapter, go back and read it now, paying particular attention to the index card example. That's a form of cash flow statement. It simply shows you over a period of time—a month at a minimum, although a year is better—how money is washing through your life, coming in as salary and going out as innumerable expenses, some of which are necessary, others of which are purely discretionary. Pay attention to what your cash flow statement tells you you're doing with your money, and I guarantee your financial situation will be much improved a year from now.

DINKs AT MIDDLE AGE

Dual incomes and no kids. But no real investment program, either. What's the problem? Many people in this situation have simply found the delights of spending money freely too attractive to give up. But now is the time to seriously reassess just how much fun that spending really is. With only twenty years—and believe me, they'll pass surprisingly quickly—before retirement, time is short to build the kind of substantial investment portfolio that will provide comfort and security for twenty or more years. Here are some numbers that will give you an idea of what you must accomplish in the next twenty years.

1. How much income will you need at retirement to live comfortably? We'll say 75 percent of your current income. If your combined salaries are $100,000, we'll call it $75,000. Now, assuming you are age forty-five, adjust it for 4 percent inflation for twenty years by multiplying $75,000 (or whatever your own number is) by 2.19. In this example the result—the amount of annual income you'll need to replicate a $75,000 income in today's dollars at age sixty-five—is $217,500. Now multiply that number by 2.19. That's the amount—$476,325—you'll need annually if you reach age eighty-five to maintain today's $75,000 standard of living.
2. How much in assets does it require to produce that

income? Well, if stocks yield about 10 percent annually, you would need $2,175,000 when you retire, and that affords absolutely no cushion for the inevitable down years in the stock market. If bonds yield 6 percent and you want the security of certain income, you'll need a portfolio of bonds worth more than $3,500,000.

3. But neither of those portfolios addresses the need for rising income to meet the burden of inflation during a twenty-year span in retirement. They also (fortunately) don't take into account the possibility of gradually whittling away at your capital to make ends meet. If you're willing to eat away at your capital, and (to be safe) you figure on a twenty-five-year span in retirement rather than twenty years, with an assumption of 4 percent annual inflation, you'll need a nest egg of $3 million in stocks at age sixty-five. That allows you to use $217,000 |in the first year and to increase your withdrawals by 4 percent annually. At the end of twenty-five years it will all be gone. At the lower 6 percent returns of an all-bond portfolio, you'll need $4.4 million at age sixty-five to meet those same goals.

Of course, the next logical question is "How the hell do we get that kind of money?" "Not easily" is the quick answer. But it also isn't impossible, especially if you're investing in stocks. Much depends on what your net worth statement reveals about what you are starting with. If the answer is "Nothing," the trip will be very difficult. To amass $3 million in a span of twenty years at a 10 percent average annual return, you would need to sock away $43,000 each year. That may be more than the after-tax earnings of either of you and would be a crushing burden, both financially and psychologically.

But let's assume you haven't been completely out of touch with financial reality and that together your 401(k) plans have accumulated $200,000, a very reasonable assumption for two people who have been in the workforce at average salaries for twenty years or more. With that as the foundation of a stock portfolio, you can assemble the necessary $3 million by adding $26,000 per year to your $200,000 base. Some of it will be added through additional contributions by you and your companies to the 401(k) plans, while the remainder comes from your after-tax earnings and is invested in mutual funds outside the 401(k) plans. The journey could be even easier if, for instance, you have enough equity in your house that it is worth refinancing it to take out some of that cash. If, for example, you could find $50,000 additional cash through refinancing, bringing your total foundation to $250,000 ($200,000 in 401(k) plans and $50,000 in home equity), you would need to add only $21,000 a year (some in 401(k) contributions, the remainder in investments outside retirement plans) to hit your $3 million target by age sixty-five. Your house obviously is an asset of some value; it will provide shelter in your retirement years, or you can convert it to cash at a considerable tax advantage compared with that of most other assets. But you'll need to live somewhere at some cost, and the returns from individual homes are volatile enough that you can't use house appreciation as an effective long-term planning tool.

Another way to go about meeting your goal is to save an increasing amount each year, which reduces the burden of saving now at the expense of forcing you to find increasing sums of money to save each year. Given your former profligate spending habits, that shouldn't be hard to do in the first few years as you pay off car loans and cut back on the purchase of clothes, dinners out, and expensive trips. But it will become increasingly difficult in later years, as salaries plateau and your spending discipline becomes firm, making it harder to find new sources of saving. Go back to the earlier scenario in which you had a combination of $200,000 in 401(k) plans. Rather than invest an additional $26,000 every year, you could invest $19,000 the first year, then increase that amount by 5 percent per year. You will actually wind up with a somewhat larger retirement kitty than if you stuck to the flat $26,000 plan. But be forewarned, your final year's contribution will be over $50,000. That kind of money isn't lying under rocks just waiting to be found.

What we just examined was how a couple could reach their retirement goals in twenty years by straining to save maximum amounts of money and investing it in stocks. Conservative investors who prefer the steadier returns of bonds simply can't, under any practical circumstances, get where they want to go without some outside intervention in the form of an inheritance or some other windfall. Their only alternative is to reduce their expected standard of living in retirement. That's hardly an inviting prospect, but just how much the reduction will be depends upon how forcefully they attack the problem of saving more money. Since you know you won't be able to provide yourself with 75 percent of your current income, adjusted for inflation, throughout your retirement years, the best approach is to calculate how much you can save each year and understand what income that amount will produce. That way you can do some advance planning about where and how you'll best live on that amount in retirement. In the worst-case scenario we'll say you're starting with essentially nothing and can, through rigorous restraint, save and invest a total of $35,000 annually, about the equivalent of one take-home salary for a couple earning a total of about $100,000 a year. At a yield of 6 percent per year, that amount invested each year over twenty years will yield a portfolio valued at $1,476,995 at age sixty-five. Calculating a retirement period of twenty-five years and continued yields of 6 percent, as well as assuming you will consume all your capital in twenty-five years, you can withdraw $73,554 in the first year of retirement and increase that amount by 4 percent in each subsequent year until, twenty-five years later, it's all gone. While that $73,554 doesn't sound so bad in today's dollars, you have to remember that inflation will be devaluing those dollars substantially between now and when you actually get them. At 4 percent annual inflation, you'll be making do on the equivalent of $34,000 of today's dollars, about one-third of what you both are earning today.

But let's look on the brighter side and assume that you've managed to build up $140,000 or so in your 401(k) plans (that's right, it's less than the $200,000 the other couple had, but you've been investing more conservatively than they have). Using that foundation and adding $35,000 more to that per year makes things look a little less appalling. You'll wind up with a portfolio of $1,813,744. Again assuming twenty-five years of retirement and that you eat up your capital over that time period, you will have an annual income of $90,324 in your first year of retirement. Unfortunately, stated in today's dollars, that would be the equivalent of $41,000, still less than half of your current total salaries.

Of course, you understand that in the examples of both the 10 percent all-stock returns and the 6 percent all-bond returns, we're looking at extremes. The more bonds you add to that stock portfolio to reduce its volatility, the less you'll ultimately have to retire on. And the more stocks you're willing to add to that conservative bond portfolio, the more you'll have to retire on. Social Security will be around, too, to provide some additional cushion, and a lot can happen, for both the better and the worse, over twenty years. The only point you need to take away from all this is the pressing urgency to address your financial situation.

You've Got Those Tuition Bill Blues

Well, if a dual-income couple without any kids is going to have a struggle to fund their retirements, what's a couple with two college-bound kids going to do? The first thing they're going to do is prioritize. No question about it, a college education is an important asset. But if you're forty-five years old and facing seven or eight years of college tuition bills that you really haven't done much to plan for, you're going to have to make some fundamental decisions:

1. Can the kids get a good education at a less expensive school? Remember our discussion in chapter 1 about opportunity costs? Apply a little of that reasoning in this situation. For every $1,000 you can trim the annual tuition bill, you'll have $6,730 more to retire on twenty years from now. Is a private college with a $15,000 annual tuition bill really three times better than the state university with a $5,000 bill? Only you can answer that question, but don't answer it without thinking through the long-term financial implications.

2. Should I borrow to finance college? From which sources? First, the reality: Borrowing to finance college educations is going to prolong the agony. Instead of eight years of money flowing out, it will be disappearing from your bank account for several years after the youngest kid has received a degree. That outflow not only costs you in financing charges, but it eats into the time any investments you make can be compounding. If someone needs to go into debt to pay for college, why not place the repayment burden on the ones whose asset the college education will be? It certainly makes more financial sense for a recent college graduate with an entire career still ahead to shoulder the debt burden (often at favorable rates applied to student loans) rather than

parents who are facing an uphill battle to gather sufficient retirement assets in what, by investment standards, is a painfully short period of time.

But if you insist on indebting yourself, there are better ways than others to go about it. First, avoid the temptation to borrow from your 401(k) plan. Although it is technically your money that you're borrowing, and you'll be repaying yourself at some stated interest rate, what you're really doing is impeding the ability of your principal retirement asset to do its job: compound at the fastest rate possible. The interest rate at which you repay your loan will almost certainly be far below the return that money would earn invested in stocks. What's more, you're repaying yourself with after-tax dollars. When you're retired and withdrawing that money, you will be taxed on it again. Paying taxes once is painful; paying taxes on the same money twice is dumb. There's also the danger that before the loan is repaid you might change jobs. If you leave your current employer, you face the prospect of either having to repay your 401(k) loan in full before you leave or having your loan treated as a premature withdrawal, which will be taxed at ordinary income rates as well as penalized an additional 10 percent. That's putting an awfully big dent in your retirement plans.

The better way is to either refinance your house or take out a home equity loan. In either case the interest you're paying will be subsidized by the government's favorable tax treatment of mortgage interest, which means it's the cheapest money you can borrow.

So we'll assume that from age forty-five to age fifty-two you've been struggling to pay tuition bills. Now, with retirement looming just thirteen years away, what's the next step? Just as our DINKs did in the earlier example, your challenge is to figure out how much you can save and invest each year to determine how much you'll have to live on in retirement. Once that's been determined, the objective is to begin designing now a retirement lifestyle (location, type of housing, and priorities for spending) that can be supported by that retirement fund. Stocks are the only viable investment vehicle to achieve any significant amount of money in thirteen years, and they will also be far and away the best vehicles to maximize income during retirement. What that means, however, is that the retirement lifestyle you're designing must be one that can accommodate the inherent volatility of stocks. Simply put, that means you'll have to live on less than the anticipated average 10 percent annual return. Any circumstances—like a prolonged bear market—that require you to dip into capital beyond the precalculated amounts that will exhaust your retirement fund in twenty-five years will jeopardize the later years of your retirement. If, for example, you experienced a 20 percent market decline one year instead of a 10 percent gain, yet you continued to withdraw money that year at the usual increasing rate, your retirement fund—assuming the market didn't restore that one year's loss in subsequent years—would run out of money several years earlier than you expected. Another option, of course, is to delay retirement and keep working. Not only does that build up your asset base, it shortens the time that retirement funds must cover. Here are some scenarios to consider.

We'll start with this premise: At age fifty-three you have between you $300,000 or so in 401(k) funds—invested in stocks, of course—to which you and your employer will continue to contribute. We'll also assume that with college payments behind you, you can now save and invest $20,000 a year outside of retirement plans. If you retire at sixty-five, your total portfolio will be worth a little more than $1.9 million. That amount will allow you to withdraw $138,000 in your first year of retirement and 4 percent more each year until the fund is exhausted after twenty-five years (again, to be on the safe side we're planning for you to live five years more than you probably will). Of course, remember that your $138,000 thirteen years from now will be worth $83,000 of today's dollars after 4 percent annual inflation.

But if you hang on until age seventy, the outlook is considerably brighter. Not only has your retirement kitty—the 401(k) as well as investments outside the plan—grown to $3.3 million, but you now calculate withdrawal rates from your retirement fund that will exhaust it in twenty years rather than twenty-five. That means you can withdraw nearly $267,000 the first year of retirement and 4 percent more each year thereafter until the fund is exhausted at age ninety. The only blight on this much rosier scenario is that inflation has sapped the value of those dollars a little more and the $267,000 is worth about $133,000 in today's dollars. But $50,000 more in real annual income will make retirement a much more pleasant state to contemplate.

In this discussion of investment possibilities for forty-five-year-old couples, we've been talking about two people with a comfortable, albeit moderate, income. If your combined family income is substantially above this level of about $100,000 per year, you may dismiss the examples as not applying to you. But from my discussions with a wide range of people over the years, I think they probably are more applicable than you assume. People with higher incomes tend to have higher spending patterns. They also have higher assumptions about how they want to live in retirement. And, in a broad sense, kids tend to pick up their parents' spending habits, so that if their parents spend freely, so do the kids. Thus a college education for the child of a relatively well-off couple who has been spending freely for much of their adult lives will cost them more than the exact same college education for the child of a more frugal couple. The kids may stay in an apartment rather than a less expensive dorm room, they'll want a late-model used car instead of a older used car (or no car at all), and they'll spend more on clothes and entertainment. So no matter what your income, take the lesson to heart: Middle age is the last chance you're likely to have to plan for a secure and comfortable retirement.

9

MAKING THE MOST
OF LIMITED TIME:

Portfolios for Your Fifties

IN SOME CASES IT'S EASIER to advise people in this age bracket about how to invest, because many of the factors that complicate financial decisions for younger people are no longer present. There aren't any kids to educate, they either have equity in a house or they're renters, and they're not trying to impress friends and neighbors with new cars or other displays of ostentation. But the hard part of advising people in this age bracket who haven't done much financial planning is that there are so few ways to build substantial amounts of capital with the very short time left to them. Those who are willing and able can continue to work for another fifteen years or so, although it's likely that the majority will remain on the job for only ten years or less. In that short span they must amass enough money to carry them through twenty years or more of retirement living. While I'm a great advocate of 401(k) plans and the control they give individuals over their financial future, I also recognize the benefits of the old-fashioned pension, or defined benefit, system. Under the defined benefit system retirees don't need to worry about how their money is invested because it won't make any difference in the amount of retirement pay they receive. The market fell 30 percent last year? Who cares? I still get my $3,000 a month. And since retirement payments under such plans are often indexed to inflation, there's not much to worry about there, either.

Once again, before we decide where to go we need to know what we have to get us there. And that means preparation of net worth and cash flow statements. We're looking at the net worth statement to find underemployed assets. The two most likely such assets are 401(k) plans and homes. The 401(k) plans present opportunities for investors to go in one of two directions at this stage of their lives. If the assets in a 401(k) are conservatively invested in fixed-income or other "safe" vehicles, which is a typical approach for people who haven't paid much attention to financial planning, now is the time to move a healthy chunk of that money into stocks, which will provide the portfolio with a little more "oomph" over the next ten years or so. But for people who have been aggressive investors over the years, with most of their assets in stocks, this is the time to consider moving toward a more conservative stance. As we'll discuss in our section on portfolios for retirees, no matter how you think about retirement, whether as a reward for hard work or as punishment because you have been so wed to your career, the sudden loss of income when you retire can be psychologically unnerving. Couple that with a portfolio that is heavily tied to the sometimes violent moves of the stock market, and personal finances can become a real source of anxiety. If you think you can weather the stock market's gyrations, that's fine. But if you think you may be upset—that's putting it lightly—by a 20 percent drop in the value of your portfolio, you have ten years to add more conservative assets to your 401(k).

The trick is to calculate—and keep calculating as these final years in the workforce pass—how much you'll need to live on in retirement and whether your chosen asset mix can get you there. I'm not talking here about moving 80 percent of your portfolio to conservative investments. With ten years of working still ahead and another twenty-five years of retirement after that, it's well worth it to risk the ups and downs of stocks to get their larger rewards. But if you move a few percent each year, you'll have a portfolio ten years from now that still has a healthy dose of stocks whose volatility is tempered by more tranquil assets. Unfortunately, few 401(k) plans offer the outright purchase of bonds as an option, so you'll have to content yourself with bond funds.

It is somewhat more important at this age to begin moving whatever investments you have outside retirement plans toward the posture you want to have when you retire. The reason is taxes.

As long as you are working with assets within a 401(k) plan, you're protected from the tax consequences of any changes in your investment posture. You could, for instance, decide at age sixty-five to roll over your entire 401(k) account, which may consist entirely of stocks, into an individual IRA that consists entirely of bonds. You wouldn't pay any capital gains taxes on the sale of the stocks, and you wouldn't pay any income taxes on the bond interest until you began withdrawing money from the plan. But try that same maneuver with assets outside retirement plans and you'll trigger a big tax bill on the capital gains of the stock portfolio, resulting in a much reduced portfolio. So if you think you'll want a more conservative posture for your investments outside of retirement plans, begin now to build a bond ladder constructed with ten-year inflation-indexed Treasury notes, using new money when possible to avoid triggering taxable gains in stock holdings. And keep in mind that if you're willing to think about your entire portfolio—401(k) plan assets as well as holdings outside retirement plans—as a single chunk of money, you want to put income-producing investments such as bonds in the 401(k) and keep stocks, which get favorable tax treatment in any case, in the taxable side of your portfolio.

UNLOCKING HOME EQUITY VALUES

A house, if you own one, can also be a powerful tool to bolster an investment plan so late in life. If you've owned the house for ten years or so, it's likely you have some equity tied up in it. While the price appreciation of residential real estate is a function of its locality, chances are that most of the country isn't enjoying—or enduring, if you're a potential buyer—the kinds of soaring valuations that property owners in places like Manhattan and San Francisco are seeing. If the price appreciation is the more typical low-single-digit annual gain, there's little question that it makes more sense financially to shift some of the equity in the house to the stock market. There are two ways to do that: refinance or sell. While it would appear at first glance that selling would be the more lucrative approach—after all, you're moving money from an asset producing a 4 percent return to one yielding 10 percent—that isn't necessarily the case.

Keep in mind that a house with a mortgage offers the owner several advantages. First, as we discussed earlier, the mortgage interest is deductible for income tax purposes, so the money you borrow against a house probably is the cheapest you'll ever get. Second, the profits you make when you eventually sell a house are tax-free up to $500,000 for a couple, providing they meet the basic IRS criteria. But finally, a house with a mortgage is a highly leveraged asset. Basically you're controlling an asset by putting down just 20 percent or so of its value. You can, for example, control a $100,000 asset by putting down only $20,000. If that asset is appreciating at 4 percent per year, you're earning $4,000 per year, but your cost has been only $20,000. That's a real return on the money you have invested of 20 percent, twice what you can expect from the stock market. Granted, you have to make monthly payments on the mortgage, but you'd have to pay monthly rent if you didn't have the house. So the somewhat startling answer is that your best course of action at age fifty-five in many cases will be to refinance the house, removing equity to invest in the stock market while continuing to control a very large asset at a minimal cost.

Start with a house you purchased twenty years ago for $150,000 with a thirty-year $120,000 mortgage. We'll say it has appreciated at an average annual rate of 4 percent, about the same as inflation. Today the house would be worth $328,500, and you would still owe $72,600 on the mortgage. Your monthly payments are $880, but if you're in the 31 percent tax bracket, you're really paying only $729 after taking into account your mortgage deduction.

Now we'll say you keep the house and the only financial step you take is to prepare a cash flow statement from which you manage to find $800 a month that you can invest in stocks in preparation for retirement ten years from now. When that day arrives, your house will be worth $486,180 and your stock portfolio will have another $193,000, for a total asset value of $679,180. And, of course, you no longer have to pay $880 a month on the mortgage. But the $486,180 in home equity, while a very nice thing to admire on paper, is essentially worthless to you in your quest to pay bills, buy groceries and gasoline, or do anything else that involves spending money. All you have to draw on for living expenses (ignoring for the moment any 401(k) assets or Social Security payments) is that $193,000 in your stock portfolio. If you plan to have it last twenty-five years, you can take out only about $14,000 the first year, an amount that will rise 4 percent per year until the fund is exhausted.

That won't work for many of us, so let's consider selling the house instead. If you do it yourselves and don't have to pay a broker, you'll walk away with the $256,000 you had in equity. Put that directly to work in the stock market, and ten years from now you'll have $665,600. Of course, you have to pay rent, but we'll say you move into an apartment that rents for about the same amount as your monthly mortgage note. You prepare your cash flow statement and still find $800 a month you can save and invest each year. That amounts, as it did in the first example, to $193,000 after ten years. Together, then, you have assets totaling $858,000, and it's all liquid. Withdrawing it at a rate that will last twenty-five years, you can take out $62,033 the first year and 4 percent each year thereafter until it's gone. If, however, your rent payments are higher than your after-tax mortgage payments, the amount you have and how much you can withdraw obviously will be less.

Finally, let's refinance 70 percent of the house's value, borrowing $230,000 at 8 percent. The house will still be worth $486,180 ten years from now. You will owe $201,700 on your mortgage, giving you equity of $284,480. Meantime, the $230,000 you took out of your house and invested in stocks has, over ten years, become $598,000. Since you have higher mortgage payments with this bigger loan, we won't give you any additional amounts to invest. The result: If you now sell the house, you will have total assets of $882,480. From that you can withdraw $63,800 the first year and 4 percent more each year thereafter.

You may be thinking that the refinancing approach yields only a little more than the outright sale of the house, and that's true. But it also allows you to stay in your house and community for another ten years, a point that will doubtless sway some people. The real lesson here, however, is that if you're facing a short time frame to amass the most money possible, you have to unlock the value of assets to let them provide the maximum return. And how to do that isn't always readily apparent.

10

UNLEASHING YOUR ASSETS:

Portfolios for Retirement

WELL, CONGRATULATIONS. You're at or near retirement. How you view being in that position depends a lot on how much pleasure you derived from your work, whether you're looking forward to liberation or boredom, and how much money you have to live on. Unfortunately, at this late date there isn't much I can do to help you accumulate a lot more money. You're going to have to make do with what you've got and what it can earn for you. You know your personal situation, including your health, much better than anyone else. But if you're an average part of statistical America, you have about twenty years still ahead of you. That's ample time to enjoy the average gains from an all-stock portfolio, provided you can weather the few bad years that one should expect in a span of two decades. But I also recognize that the absence of a regular salary can produce psychological, if not real financial, anxieties. That's why it is probably wise at this point to think carefully about the structure that you want your retirement portfolio to have as you embark on the retired phase of your life. No matter how conservative or aggressive you were with your investments while you were working and enjoying regular paychecks, you're probably going to want to be more conservative now. And by conservative I don't just mean skewing your portfolio more toward bonds and away from stocks. I'm also talking about the spending side of your life. The two actually go hand in hand, since the adoption of a more conservative investment posture has as a corollary a reduction in the amount of money to spend. Having said that, I think it's also necessary to ask you to carefully consider the spending side of the cash flow equation, even if you have an all-stock portfolio, simply to be certain you have the cushion you need for the years in which stock market returns are lower than average or negative.

Here's an example of what I mean. It isn't uncommon for people nearing retirement age these days to have a retirement portfolio worth $1 million. Invested in an asset earning an average of 10 percent per year, you could take out $80,900 in the first year, increase that amount 4 percent each year thereafter, and run out of money twenty years from now. That same $1 million invested in a fixed-income portfolio yielding 6 percent would allow you to withdraw $59,600 the first year and 4 percent more each year thereafter, and you will also run out of money twenty years from now. But if you invest in stocks while living on a budget that would be produced by bonds, your assets would be growing each year, by $21,300 in the first year, and that amount would rise each year at a rate somewhat in excess of 4 percent. At the end of twenty years you would have ample assets to continue living on or to pass on to heirs. Meanwhile, you could draw down your stock portfolio to cover any shortfall in the bad years. Another way to accomplish the same goal is to set up your asset base—your 401(k) portfolio as well as any other investments outside of retirement plans—to meet your living expenses while investing your Social Security checks in stock funds. This situation is, of course, something of a luxury. But it emphasizes what can be done if you can find reasonable savings in your cash flow.

If you choose to move toward a more conservative stance with your investment portfolio, concentrate on making any changes in your 401(k) plan, not in your outside investments. That way you avoid being taxed. If, for example, you suddenly were to convert a portfolio of stocks worth $500,000 to bonds outside your 401(k), the taxes would take a heavy toll on the overall size of the portfolio. That same transaction done within a 401(k) would have no immediate tax implications.

MORE STRATEGIES FOR UNLOCKING HOME EQUITY

We discussed in the section on portfolios for couples in their fifties the possibility of their unlocking the equity built up on a house to bolster the performance of an investment portfolio if it looked as if they might fall short of their retirement goals. The best step they could take was to refinance their home with a much larger mortgage. But that particular solution relied heavily on the fact that they still had income from which to meet the higher mortgage payments. It isn't likely that if you're in need of more capital to produce retirement income, you will be in a position to shoulder higher mortgage payments. Yet the equity in your house could be enormously helpful in meeting your financial needs if it could be put to work earning better returns. That means selling the house (remember, there are no taxes on the gains for most people selling their primary residence) and renting or buying something that costs substantially less. Let's explore some of these options to see what turns up.

The basic assumption is that you have a house worth $300,000 and you've paid off the mortgage, so you'll take $300,000 away if you sell it. While the house may be appreciating at a few percent per year, that doesn't help you because it produces no income. The only advantage to holding on to the house is that you no longer have to make a house payment (although you still must pay local taxes). Your other options are to sell it and rent something, sell it and buy something smaller for cash, or sell it and buy something cheaper with a mortgage. The results of this exercise will change as you shift variables. But keeping all other things equal, here's what happens in each case.

• Sell the house and rent. Putting $300,000 in an all-stock portfolio produces average annual gains of $30,000, which, after capital gains taxes (let's say 14 percent), leaves you with additional income of $25,800 over what you had before you sold the house. Investing the home sale proceeds in bonds yielding 6 percent gives you additional gross income of $18,000, which, taxed at 28 percent, leaves you $12,960. If you rent something for $1,200 a month, or $14,400 a year, you can see that you'll be better off if you've invested your home sale proceeds in stocks, but worse off if they're in bonds. Reduce that monthly rent to $800, or $9,600 a year, and you gain in both categories, although the $16,200 surplus from stocks looks substantially more appealing than the $3,360 excess from bonds.

• Sell the house and buy a condo for $100,000 in cash. Now you have $200,000 to invest, which returns $17,200 after taxes in stocks and $8,640 in bonds. Condo fees may cost $2,000 a year, but you're still nicely ahead with either stocks or bonds than you would have been if you hadn't sold the house.

  • Finally, sell the house and buy a condo for $100,000 with 20 percent down and an $80,000 mortgage at 8 percent. Now you have $280,000 to invest, which returns $24,080 after taxes when invested in stocks and $12,096 in bonds. With your mortgage interest income tax deduction, your annual housing cost, including condo fees, is $7,253. Thus you're better off by $16,827 if you're invested in stocks and by $4,843 if you're invested in bonds.

Again, you can change the variables and get different results, but the point remains: A lot of hidden value is locked up in home equity. If you don't need to tap it and love your home, that's fine. But if you need additional money to make retirement comfortable or just tolerable, one of the first places to turn for help is your home.

We've covered a lot of ground in this portfolio section of the book. I hope I've provided you with at least a few ideas about how to maximize your own saving and investing program. In any event, following is a brief summary of all we've discussed, indicating where most people usually are at various stages of life and where they should be in an ideal world. Don't use it as an instruction manual, merely as one of several measures you can use to put your own financial situation into perspective.

Portfolio Summary:
Ages 25 Through 65

Age 25

Ideal: Full 401(k) contributions in diverse stock funds; regular investments in taxable stock funds; possibly some savings in money market accounts for down payment on house five years away. Great time to get an early start on amassing wealth.

Likely: Some 401(k) participation split between stocks and "safe" investments; no other regular investment program. Unlikely to be very concerned about building wealth.

Age 35

Ideal: Full 401(k) participation; continuing regular investments in taxable stock funds; home equity beginning to build; possibly college education money being diverted to money market account or (preferably) to stocks; preparation of net worth statement and analysis of cash flow; couples without children may begin to consider possible lifestyle changes, including early retirement.

Likely: Some 401(k) participation split between stocks and "safe" investments; home equity beginning to build; no regular investment program beyond putting some money into savings accounts for college; no clear knowledge of net worth or cash flow.

Age 45

Ideal: Full 401(k) participation; college educations being financed from stock portfolio that continues to grow; some regular investments in stocks continue; home equity builds; net worth growing and cash flow positive.

Likely: Some 401(k) participation; college educations being financed partially by savings, partially by loans, including home equity loan; no regular investments being made; net worth stagnant, cash flow neutral or negative.

Age 55

Ideal: Full participation in 401(k) with some investors beginning to shift balance of investments toward conservative posture; continued regular investments in taxable stock funds; possible refinancing of home to unlock accumulated equity; preliminary planning for retirement; net worth growing rapidly and cash flow solidly positive; couples without children may be retired at this point.

Likely: Full participation in 401(k) as looming retirement induces financial anxiety; some preliminary retirement planning; net worth growing moderately and cash flow positive; home equity continues to build.

Age 65

Ideal: Retirement income from combination of stocks and bonds in both 401(k) and taxable accounts comfortably in excess of needs; home equity may be building anew after earlier refinancing or may be redeployed to less costly home in new location; net worth growing moderately and cash flow positive.

Likely: Retirement income from mostly conservative investments adequate with some capital drain; home may be fully paid off with equity sitting idle; net worth stagnant or slowly declining, cash flow modestly negative.

EPILOGUE:

The Value of Time and Money

CAN IT REALLY BE THIS EASY AND THIS GOOD?

Can you, acting on your own without any contact with brokers, money managers, or professional investment advisers, really build an investment portfolio worth millions of dollars using just index funds and Treasury bonds?

You bet!

All you have to do is follow the basic guidelines I've outlined in this book. Develop a conscientious approach to saving money. Invest a big chunk of that money you save in a diversified stock portfolio consisting of low-cost index funds. Then simply be patient as the power of compounding returns builds your fortune over the years.

It really is that easy and that good.

But only if you stick to the program. And that may not be so easy to do. You're embarking on a lifelong process, and there are going to be pitfalls along the way that tempt you to deviate from the approach I've set out here. First, you're going to be surrounded for the rest of your life by people telling you how complicated investing is and how you need professional advice. A lot of them are going to want you to pay them for that advice. They're going to talk about all sorts of complicated strategies and techniques for making lots of money fast, and they're going to laugh at you for being such a simpleton as to think index funds are really a smart investment tool.

What they don't know is that you're now armed with knowledge. You know, for example, that there will always be investment managers who beat the market. But you also know that neither you nor anyone else can pick them in advance. You know, too, that very, very few of them will be able to beat the market consistently over the course of your entire lifetime. And that's the only game worth playing.

There also will be times when the financial markets aren't doing well and you'll question the wisdom of being invested in stocks. But since you now know that even at the worst times in the past—and hopefully none of us will ever experience anything as bad as the Great Depression—stocks remained the best long-term investment, you will have the faith and discipline to stick with your portfolio instead of caving in to fear. There will be other times when the markets are doing fabulously well and you question why you're not getting the fantastic returns that you read or hear about others making. But since you now know that the people getting those huge returns are taking huge risks to do so and that it is unlikely the returns will persist for more than a few years at best, you will be able to take quiet satisfaction in the much steadier and more reliable returns of a well-diversified portfolio. And you also know about the serenity and security that come with being the master of your finances rather than a slave to debt or whim.

Any worthwhile lifelong endeavor—career, family, hobbies—requires both patience and flexibility. The same is true of investing. I'm convinced that the approach I've outlined in this book is the best way to invest for a lifetime. But I don't want you to be rigid about it. Sure, saving money is important. But don't let your urge to save get in the way of spending money on things that are truly important, such as family vacations, recreation, and education. As I warned earlier, the worst thing you can do is adopt such a strenuous savings program that you deny yourself and your loved ones too much and finally decide to abandon the whole project. Index funds certainly are the most efficient way to build a diversified portfolio, but don't feel you're violating some law if you want to try your hand at a little stock picking from time to time. And don't be unreceptive to other investment opportunities beyond stocks and bonds. My father-in-law has turned his knowledge of old houses and commercial buildings into a lucrative investment sideline over the years. But it has worked only because he knows enough about construction, renovation, and land values to make informed judgments for himself rather than rely on real estate brokers or others who will make money whether he does or not.

Above all, take advantage of the simplicity of this investment approach. If you find investing as fascinating as some people do, fine, make it something of a hobby. But if other things interest you more—coaching the kids' soccer team, hiking the Appalachian Trail, cooking gourmet meals—you can freely engage in any or all of them without feeling the least bit of guilt about neglecting your finances or missing the least percentage point of performance. That's because this approach not only gives you the best returns, it also gives you more of that most precious commodity of all—time.

An Investor's Tool Kit

HERE ARE FOUR TOOLS THAT CAN BE very helpful in getting you where you want to go as a lifelong investor. The first two direct you to the right places to set up your mutual fund and Treasury bond investments. The last two allow you to do some "what if" planning, an essential component of investing for such goals as college and retirement. For those of you with access to the Internet, I've provided interactive tools to test various financial scenarios at www.winning.wsj.com.

1. THE WORLD'S BEST INDEX FUNDS

There's nothing simpler than index investing, and I'm going to make it even simpler. Here's a list of index funds from which you can build a very effective lifetime investment portfolio. Although there are dozens of index funds, this list is focused only on those with low expenses and reasonable minimum investments. If you buy any other index funds, you'll probably be paying too much and hurting your returns. Certainly you should always avoid those with the gall to charge loads. The list isn't long, and as you can see, it's dominated by Vanguard, which shouldn't be surprising. John Bogle, Vanguard's founder, pioneered the concept of index investing. In addition, Vanguard's unique corporate structure, in which the investment companies that manage the various funds jointly own the Vanguard Group, allows the Vanguard Group to provide management, administrative, and marketing services to the funds at cost. As a result, Vanguard consistently has the lowest expense ratios in the mutual fund industry. And since index funds should perform similarly—with the exception of costs—Vanguard typically has superior performance. It also keeps minimum investments low enough to allow almost anyone to invest in its funds.

You can use the one-stop shopping list to set up a global stock portfolio using just two funds (or a broad-based U.S. portfolio using just one fund), or you can use the "Mix and Match" list to construct your own customized portfolio of index funds. Keep in mind that you want a degree of diversity in your portfolio that spreads the risk around a broad group of stocks. You don't, for instance, want to put your entire portfolio in emerging markets stocks. Rather, you might want to have 10 percent or so in emerging markets while the rest is spread around other U.S. and foreign funds.

Finally, I've given you a list that consists of funds that I consider "second best," in case you simply don't like Vanguard.

ONE-STOP SHOPPING

These funds provide extremely broad exposure to their target markets, making it unnecessary to seek further diversification.

U.S. STOCKS

Vanguard Total Stock Market Index Fund
    Target: Wilshire 5000 index
    Expense ratio: 0.20%
    Additional fees or expenses: $2.50 quarterly account maintenance fee on accounts under $10,000
    Minimum investment: $3,000; $1,000 for IRAs and custodial accounts for minors.

Fidelity Spartan Total Market Index Fund
    Target: Wilshire 5000 index
    Expense ratio: 0.27% (currently voluntarily capped at 0.25%)
    Additional fees or expenses: 0.50% short-term trading fee on shares held less than ninety days; $10 annual account maintenance fee on accounts under $10,000
    Minimum investment: $15,000

FOREIGN STOCKS

Vanguard Total International Stock Index

Target: Consists of proportional holdings in Vanguard's European, Pacific, and Emerging Market Index Funds, each of which tracks a regional index run by Morgan Stanley Capital International (see following descriptions of each fund's targets)

Expense ratio: While the fund has no direct expenses, it bears the expenses of the three separate funds in which it invests; such indirect expenses totaled 0.34% in 1999

Additional fees or expenses: $10 annual account maintenance fee for accounts under $10,000

Minimum initial investment: $3,000; $1,000 for IRAs and custodial accounts for minors

Vanguard Tax Managed International Fund (especially useful for investors with high incomes; not intended for IRA or other tax-deferred accounts)

Target: Morgan Stanley Capital International Europe, Australasia, and Far East Index

Expense ratio: 0.35%

Additional fees or expenses: A 0.25% transaction fee is charged on purchases (except dividend and capital gains reinvestments) and is paid to the fund to defer the high costs of transactions abroad so that existing shareholders do not bear those costs; a 2% redemption fee is charged on shares held less than one year; and a 1% redemption fee is charged on shares held at least one year but less than five years. The transaction and redemption fees are intended to protect long-term investors and discourage short-term trading, which impairs the fund's tax efficiency.

Minimum initial investment: $10,000

Fidelity Spartan International Index Fund

Target: Morgan Stanley Capital International Europe, Australasia and Far East index

Expense ratio: 0.36%

Additional fees or expenses: 1% short-term trading fee for

shares held less than ninety days; $10 annual account maintenance fee for accounts under $10,000 ·
Minimum investment: $15,000

MIX AND MATCH

LARGE U.S. STOCKS

Vanguard 500 Index Fund
Target: S&P 500 index
Expense ratio: 0.18%
Additional fees or expenses: $2.50 quarterly account maintenance charge on accounts under $10,000
Minimum investment: $3,000; $1,000 for IRAs and custodial accounts for minors

Fidelity Spartan 500 Fund
Target: S&P 500 index
Expense ratio: 0.19% (voluntarily reduced; could be increased without notice)
Additional fees or expenses: 0.50% short-term trading fee on shares held less than ninety days; $10 annual account maintenance fee on accounts of less than $10,000
Minimum investment: $10,000; $500 for retirement accounts

SSGA S&P 500 Index Fund
Target: S&P 500 index
Expense ratio: 0.18% (artificially capped)
Minimum investment: $10,000

MIDCAP AND SMALL-CAP U.S. STOCKS

Vanguard Extended Market Index Fund
Target: Wilshire 4500 ("Completion Index")
Expense ratio: 0.25%
Additional fees or expenses: $10 annual account maintenance fee for accounts less than $2,500
Minimum investment: $3,000; $1,000 for IRAs and custodial accounts for minors

Fidelity Spartan Extended Market Index Fund
    Target: Wilshire 4500 ("Completion Index")
    Expense ratio: 0.31% (currently voluntarily capped at
      0.25%)
    Additional fees or expenses: 0.75% short-term trading fee on
      shares held less than ninety days; $10 annual account
      maintenance fee on accounts of less than $10,000
    Minimum investment: $15,000

MIDCAP U.S. STOCKS

Vanguard MidCap Index Fund
    Target: S&P MidCap 400 index
    Expense ratio: 0.25%
    Additional fees or expenses: $10 annual account mainte-
      nance fee on accounts less than $10,000
    Minimum investment: $3,000; $1,000 for IRAs and custo-
      dial accounts

SMALL-CAP U.S. STOCKS

Vanguard Small Cap Index Fund
    Target: Russell 2000 index
    Expense ratio: 0.25%
    Additional fees or expenses: $10 annual account mainte-
      nance fee for accounts less than $10,000; although no
      transaction fees are currently charged, the fund has re-
      served the right to charge such fees from future pur-
      chases; transaction fees are paid directly to the fund to
      protect existing shareholders from the costs of new in-
      vestors
    Minimum investment: $3,000; $1,000 for IRAs and custo-
      dial accounts for minors

Vanguard Tax Managed Small Cap Fund (especially useful to
investors with high incomes; not intended for retirement plans)
    Target: S&P SmallCap 600 index
    Expense ratio: 0.19%
    Additional fees or expenses: A 0.50% transaction fee is
      charged on new purchases (except from reinvested divi-
      dends and capital gains) and paid to the fund to defer the

expense of investing in small-cap stocks so that existing shareholders do not bear that expense; a 2% redemption fee is charged on shares held less than one year; and a 1% redemption fee is charged on shares held more than one year but less than five years. The transaction and redemption fees are intended to protect long-term shareholders and discourage short-term trading, which impairs the fund's tax efficiency.
Minimum investment: $10,000

FOREIGN REGIONAL STOCKS

Vanguard European Stock Index Fund
Target: Morgan Stanley Capital International Europe index
Expense ratio: 0.29%
Additional fees or expenses: A $10 annual account maintenance fee is charged on accounts of less than $10,000
Minimum investment: $3,000; $1,000 for IRAs and custodial accounts for minors

Vanguard Pacific Index Fund (more than 80% of this fund's assets are invested in Japanese stocks)
Target: Morgan Stanley Capital International Pacific free index
Expense ratio: 0.37%
Additional fees or expenses: A $10 annual account maintenance fee is charged on accounts of less than $10,000
Minimum investment: $3,000; $1,000 for IRAs and custodial accounts for minors

Vanguard Emerging Markets Fund
Target: Morgan Stanley Capital International Select Emerging Markets free index (created and administered exclusively for Vanguard by MSCI)
Expense ratio: 0.58%
Additional fees or expenses: A 0.50% transaction fee on purchases (except reinvestment of dividends and capital gains) and a 0.50% redemption fee on all sales or exchanges are charged to discourage frequent trading and to ensure that long-term investors do not carry the burden of high transaction costs in emerging markets; a $10 annual

account maintenance fee is charged on accounts of less
than $10,000

Minimum investment: $3,000; $1,000 for IRAs and custodial accounts for minors

"SECOND BEST" FUNDS

Don't like Vanguard for some reason? Here's a list of funds that
could serve as alternatives, although their expense ratios are
higher. Keep in mind that while the difference between an expense ratio of 0.18 percent and 0.40 percent doesn't seem like
much, the higher-cost fund actually costs *more than twice* as much
as the lower-cost fund. And costs count!

ONE-STOP SHOPPING

U.S. STOCKS

Schwab Total Stock Market Index Fund
Target: Wilshire 5000 index
Expense ratio: 0.40% (expenses are higher, but the fund has
voluntarily capped the expenses through February 2001)
Additional fees or expenses: 0.75% short-term trading fee
charged on shares held less than 180 days
Minimum investment: $2,500

T. Rowe Price Total Market Index Fund
Target: Wilshire 5000 index
Expense ratio: 0.40%
Minimum investment: $2,500; $1,000 for retirement
accounts

FOREIGN STOCKS

Schwab International Index Fund
Target: Schwab International index, consisting of stocks of
the 350 largest companies outside the United States
Expense ratio: 0.58% (artificially capped)
Additional fees or expenses: 1.50% redemption fee on shares
held less than 180 days

Minimum investment: $2,500; $1,000 for retirement accounts

MIX AND MATCH

LARGE-CAP U.S. STOCKS

Schwab S&P 500 Fund
Target: Standard & Poor's 500 stock index
Expense ratio: 0.35% (artificially capped)
Minimum investment: $2,500; $1,000 for retirement
accounts

Schwab 1000 Fund
Target: Schwab 1000 index of the one thousand largest U.S.
companies by market capitalization
Expense ratio: 0.46% (artificially capped)
Additional fees or expenses: 0.50% redemption fee; 0.75%
redemption fee on shares held less than 180 days
Minimum investment: $2,500; $1,000 for retirement
accounts

SMALL-CAP U.S. STOCKS

Schwab Small-Cap Index Fund
Target: Schwab Small-Cap index of the second thousand
largest U.S. companies by market capitalization
Expense ratio: 0.49% (artificially capped)
Additional fees or expenses: 0.75% redemption fee on shares
held less than 180 days
Minimum investment: $2,500; $1,000 for retirement
accounts

2. SETTING UP A TREASURY DIRECT ACCOUNT

Setting up a Treasury Direct account is easy, but be sure that
you request the paperwork in plenty of time for your account to
be established before the auction in which you want to partici-

pate is scheduled. The forms can be downloaded from the site www.publicdebt.treas.gov, or you can use the following table to determine which Federal Reserve bank to call to request forms or get help. The table is organized according to your zip code, specifically the first three digits of the code. If, for example, you lived near me in Vero Beach, Florida, your zip code would be 32963. To discover which Federal Reserve branch bank to call, simply scan through the table to find 329, the first three digits of the code. You would learn that your account will be handled by the Federal Reserve branch in Jacksonville.

If the First Three Digits of Your Zip Code Are:	Call or Write:
006–009 066 068–079 088–139	Federal Reserve Bank (New York) Federal Reserve P.O. Station New York, NY 10045-0001 (212) 720-6619 (212) 720-5823 (recording)
010–065 067	Federal Reserve Bank (Boston) Treasury Direct P.O. Box 2076 Boston, MA 02106-2076 (617) 973-3800 (recording)
080–087 166–199	Federal Reserve Bank (Philadelphia) P.O. Box 90 Philadelphia, PA 19105-0090 (215) 574-6680 (215) 574-6580 (recording)
140–149	Federal Reserve Bank (Buffalo) P.O. Box 961 Buffalo, NY 14240-0961 (716) 849-5000 (716) 849-5158

200–209	Capital Area Servicing Center
220–223	Bureau of the Public Debt
	Department N
	Washington, DC 20239-1500
224–253	Federal Reserve Bank (Richmond)
255–259	P.O. Box 27622
	Richmond, VA 23261-7622
	(804) 697-8372
	(804) 697-8355 (recording)
300–319	Federal Reserve Bank (Atlanta)
373–374	P.O. Box 662
	Atlanta, GA 30301-0662
	(404) 521-8653
	(404) 521-8657
320–329	Federal Reserve Bank (Jacksonville)
335–338	P.O. Box 2499
342	Jacksonville, FL 32231-2499
344	(904) 632-1179
346–347	(904) 632-1178 (recording)
330–334	Federal Reserve Bank (Miami)
339–340	P.O. Box 520847
349	Miami, FL 33152-0847
	(305) 471-6497
	(305) 471-6257 (recording)
350–364	Federal Reserve Bank (Birmingham)
367–368	1801 Fifth Ave. N
	Birmingham, AL 35203-2104
	(205) 731-8708
	(205) 731-8702 (recording)
403–405	Federal Reserve Bank (Cincinnati)
407–418	P.O. Box 999
425–426	Cincinnati, OH 45201-0999
450–457	(513) 455-4334
470	
472–473	

430–438	Federal Reserve Bank (Cleveland)
440–449	P.O. Box 6387
458	Cleveland, OH 44101-1387
	(216) 579-2000
	(216) 579-2490 (recording)
460–469	Federal Reserve Bank (Chicago)
500–509	P.O. Box 834
512–514	Chicago, IL 60690-0834
520–528	(312) 322-5369
530–539	(312) 322-2202 (recording)
541–543	
549	
600–619	
625–627	
480–497	Federal Reserve Bank (Detroit)
	P.O. Box 1059
	Detroit, MI 48231-1059
	(313) 964-6157
	(313) 964-6140 (recording)
150–165	Federal Reserve Bank (Minneapolis)
210–219	Treasury Direct
254	P.O. Box 9150
260–268	Minneapolis, MN 55480-9150
270–299	(612) 204-6650
380–383	
386–389	
397	
400–402	
406	
420–424	
427	
439	
474–479	
498–499	
540	
544–548	
550–599	

620–624
628–639
650–652
654–658
716–729
755

365–366	Federal Reserve Bank (Dallas)
369–372	Treasury Direct
376–379	P.O. Box 660657
384–385	Dallas, TX 75266-0657
390–396	(214) 922-6100
510–511	(214) 922-6700 (recording)
515–516	
640–648	
653	
660–693	
700–708	
710–714	
730–731	
734–741	
749–754	
756–769	
779–794	
797–816	
820–834	
836–837	
840–847	
878–884	
893	
898	
980–993	
995–999	

770–778	Federal Reserve Bank (Houston)
	P.O. Box 2578
	Houston, TX 77252-2578
	(713) 652-1621 or 1629
	(713) 652-1688 (recording)

835	Federal Reserve Bank (Portland)
838	P.O. Box 3436
970–979	Portland, OR 97208-3436
994	(503) 221-5932
	(503) 221-5931 (recording)

850–865	Federal Reserve Bank (Los Angeles)
870–877	P.O. Box 512077
890–891	Los Angeles, CA 90051-0077
900–935	(213) 624-7398

894–897	Federal Reserve Bank (San Francisco)
936–969	P.O. Box 7702
	San Francisco, CA 94120-7702
	(415) 974-2330
	(415) 974-3491 (recording)

3. HOW MUCH CAN YOU SAVE?
THE POWER OF COMPOUNDING

The following table can be a powerful tool in planning your investment portfolio. First, it demonstrates very clearly the powerful effects of compounding over time. But it also can show the insidious impact of inflation and taxes. Here's how to use it to do that and more.

The table shows how much a single dollar will grow to become if invested at different rates of return over different periods of time. For example, $1 invested at 10 percent (find the column labeled 10 percent) will become $2.85 over eleven years (find the Years Invested row labeled 11 and follow it across until it intersects the 10% Rate of Return column). All you need to do to find how much other sums will grow to become is simply multiply whatever sum you choose by the figure in the intersection of the returns column and the years row. Let's say, for example, that you have a $55,000 investment and want to know what it would be worth eleven years from now if you invest it at 10 percent. That's the same example I just used, so go to the intersection of the 10 percent Rate of Return column and the 11 Years Invested row and find 2.85. Multiply your original investment ($55,000) by that number and you find you'll have $156,750.

How do you make assumptions about rates of return? There isn't much you can do beyond relying on history. Assume a broad portfolio of stocks will earn an average of 12 percent annually over a long period of time, bonds will yield about 6 percent, and inflation will run about 3 percent. If, like me, you want to subtract a fudge factor from those historical rates to provide a little margin of safety and to reflect transaction costs, you might wind up assuming a 10 percent annual return from stocks, 5 percent from bonds, and inflation at 4 percent. To project realistic values for your entire investment portfolio, you must take into account the mix of investments you're holding. If, for example, you have $100,000 in stocks and $50,000 in bonds, you should calculate the projected returns of the two asset classes separately, then add the results.

Then there's inflation. If you're using the historical figure for inflation, merely subtract that from the historical return of stocks or bonds. Your 12 percent annual historical return on stocks thus becomes 9 percent, and the 6 percent return on bonds becomes 3 percent; use those respective columns to find how big your portfolio will become. Using the fudge factors, your rate of return on stocks becomes 6 percent, and that on bonds is reduced to a mere 1 percent. If you want to see a very graphic and scary demonstration of inflation's effects, make an assumption about what rate of return you'll earn that doesn't take into account either inflation or taxes. Using whatever initial investment sum you wish, calculate what it will be worth over any given period of time. Now do that same calculation, but this time reduce your assumed rate of return by whatever inflation rate you wish. The difference between the first calculation and the second is the penalty inflation will exact. Frightening, isn't it?

For investments held outside of such tax-advantaged plans as 401(k)s and IRAs, you might also want to take into account the impact of taxes. Taxes sap the returns from bonds much more than the returns from stocks, since bond income is a steady stream of money that is taxed at ordinary income tax rates, while stock returns are generally taxed at the lower long-term capital gains rate, and then only when the stock is sold. To determine how taxes will affect the returns from your bonds (assuming they aren't tax-

Rate of Return

Years Invested	1%	2%	3%	4%	5%	6%	7%	8%	9%	10%	11%	12%
1	1.01	1.02	1.03	1.04	1.05	1.06	1.07	1.08	1.09	1.10	1.11	1.12
2	1.02	1.04	1.06	1.08	1.10	1.12	1.14	1.17	1.19	1.21	1.23	1.25
3	1.03	1.06	1.09	1.12	1.16	1.19	1.23	1.26	1.30	1.33	1.37	1.40
4	1.04	1.08	1.13	1.17	1.22	1.26	1.31	1.36	1.41	1.46	1.52	1.57
5	1.05	1.10	1.16	1.22	1.28	1.34	1.40	1.47	1.54	1.61	1.69	1.76
6	1.06	1.13	1.19	1.27	1.34	1.42	1.50	1.59	1.68	1.77	1.87	1.97
7	1.07	1.15	1.23	1.32	1.40	1.50	1.61	1.71	1.83	1.95	2.08	2.21
8	1.08	1.17	1.27	1.37	1.48	1.59	1.72	1.85	1.99	2.14	2.30	2.48
9	1.09	1.20	1.30	1.42	1.55	1.69	1.84	2.00	2.17	2.36	2.56	2.77
10	1.10	1.22	1.34	1.48	1.63	1.79	1.97	2.16	2.37	2.60	2.84	3.11
11	1.12	1.24	1.38	1.54	1.71	1.90	2.10	2.33	2.58	2.85	3.15	3.48
12	1.13	1.27	1.43	1.60	1.80	2.01	2.25	2.52	2.81	3.14	3.50	3.90
13	1.14	1.29	1.47	1.67	1.89	2.13	2.41	2.72	3.07	3.45	3.88	4.36
14	1.15	1.32	1.51	1.73	1.98	2.26	2.58	2.94	3.34	3.80	4.31	4.89
15	1.16	1.35	1.56	1.80	2.08	2.40	2.76	3.17	3.64	4.18	4.78	5.47
16	1.17	1.37	1.60	1.87	2.18	2.54	2.95	3.43	3.97	4.60	5.31	6.13
17	1.18	1.40	1.65	1.95	2.29	2.69	3.16	3.70	4.33	5.05	5.90	6.87
18	1.20	1.43	1.70	2.03	2.41	2.85	3.38	4.00	4.72	5.56	6.54	7.69
19	1.21	1.46	1.75	2.11	2.53	3.03	3.62	4.32	5.14	6.12	7.26	8.61
20	1.22	1.49	1.81	2.19	2.65	3.21	3.87	4.66	5.60	6.73	8.06	9.65
21	1.23	1.52	1.86	2.28	2.79	3.40	4.14	5.03	6.11	7.40	8.95	10.80
22	1.24	1.55	1.92	2.37	2.93	3.60	4.43	5.44	6.66	8.14	9.93	12.10
23	1.26	1.58	1.97	2.46	3.07	3.82	4.74	5.87	7.26	8.95	11.03	13.55
24	1.27	1.61	2.03	2.56	3.23	4.05	5.07	6.34	7.91	9.85	12.24	15.18
25	1.28	1.64	2.09	2.67	3.39	4.29	5.43	6.85	8.62	10.83	13.59	17.00
26	1.30	1.67	2.16	2.77	3.56	4.55	5.81	7.40	9.40	11.92	15.08	19.04
27	1.31	1.71	2.22	2.88	3.73	4.82	6.21	7.99	10.25	13.11	16.74	21.32
28	1.32	1.74	2.29	3.00	3.92	5.11	6.65	8.63	11.17	14.42	18.58	23.88
29	1.33	1.78	2.36	3.12	4.12	5.42	7.11	9.32	12.17	15.86	20.62	26.75
30	1.35	1.81	2.43	3.24	4.32	5.74	7.61	10.06	13.27	17.45	22.90	29.96

exempt municipal bonds), you need to know your marginal tax rate. Currently, rates are set at 15 percent, 28 percent, 31 percent, 36 percent, or 39.6 percent, depending upon your income and filing status. To make things easier, round off those brackets to 15 percent, 30 percent, and 40 percent. If you're in the 30 percent bracket, for example, you should reduce your expected return by 30 percent. That means the 6 percent you expect will be only 4.2 percent (70 percent of 6 percent) after taxes. Only then should you apply your inflation adjustment. If it's the historical 3 percent, your bond returns are now totaling just 1.2 percent. And, heaven forbid, if you assume inflation at 4 percent, you're losing purchasing power on your bond portfolio. See why I prefer stocks?

4. HOW MUCH CAN YOU SPEND?
WITHDRAWING MONEY IN RETIREMENT

One of the most frightening aspects of retirement is whether you will outlive your financial resources. You probably won't if you've done a little planning and are willing to adjust your lifestyle to whatever retirement resources you have. Here are two handy little tables that give you a look at what you can reasonably expect to live on each year with a given sum of money. Once you make assumptions about the rate of return you expect from your assets and the length of time you expect to be retired, the factors in these tables tell you how much you can withdraw each year until your nest egg is exhausted. The top table gives you factors for calculating withdrawals of the same amount each year. The second table provides you with factors that tell you how much you can withdraw the first year and then allow you to increase that amount 4 percent for every year thereafter to keep pace with inflation.

Using the tables is easy. Let's say you have a retirement fund of $500,000 on which you expect to earn a 10 percent return, and you want your money to last twenty-five years. Using the top table for fixed withdrawals, simply go across the 25 Years Retired row to the 10% Expected Return column and you find the factor 0.1002. Now multiply your $500,000 nest egg by that factor and you find you can withdraw $50,100 per year. At the end of twenty-five years your money will be gone. Of course, if your returns are worse than expected, you'll have to make do with less income, and in any case your returns almost certainly will vary from one year to another. But if, on average, they're better than you expected you can spend a little more or plan to have a little cushion in case you live longer than you expect. Keep in mind that these are pretax numbers and that the top table doesn't allow you anything extra to compensate for inflation.

The bottom table, which does compensate for inflation at an average annual rate of 4 percent, works essentially the same way. The difference is that the amount you calculate using the table is the first-year withdrawal only. Each year thereafter you can increase the amount withdrawn by 4 percent. Let's use the same numbers we used a moment ago: a $500,000 retirement kitty earning 10 percent per year that must last twenty-five years. Using the second table, we find that the 10 percent return and the twenty-

Fixed Withdrawals
Expected Return

Years Retired	6%	7%	8%	9%	10%	11%	12%
15	0.0971	0.1026	0.1082	0.1138	0.1195	0.1253	0.1311
20	0.0822	0.0822	0.0943	0.1005	0.1068	0.1131	0.1195
25	0.0738	0.0802	0.0867	0.0934	0.1002	0.1070	0.1138
30	0.0685	0.0753	0.0822	0.0893	0.0964	0.1036	0.1108
35	0.0651	0.0722	0.0794	0.0868	0.0943	0.1017	0.1092
40	0.0627	0.0701	0.0776	0.0853	0.0930	0.1006	0.1083

Inflation-Adjusted Withdrawals
(Assumes 4% Annual Increases in Withdrawals)
Expected Return

Years Retired	6%	7%	8%	9%	10%	11%	12%
15	0.0759	0.0807	0.0857	0.0907	0.0959	0.1011	0.1065
20	0.0596	0.0646	0.0699	0.0753	0.0809	0.0866	0.0924
25	0.0498	0.0551	0.0606	0.0664	0.0723	0.0785	0.0847
30	0.0433	0.0489	0.0547	0.0607	0.0670	0.0735	0.0801
35	0.0388	0.0445	0.0505	0.0569	0.0635	0.0702	0.0772
40	0.0354	0.0413	0.0475	0.0541	0.0610	0.0681	0.0753

five-year duration give us a factor of 0.0723. Multiply your $500,000 fund by that factor and the answer is $36,150. That's how much you can withdraw the first year of retirement. But in the second year, to keep pace with inflation, you can increase that amount by 4 percent to $37,596. The third year the amount rises another 4 percent to $39,100. You'll note, of course, that the amount this method allows you to withdraw is substantially lower in the early years than with the level income method. In fact, this inflation-adjusted method won't equal the annual withdrawals under the level income method until the tenth year. *But*, in the last years the inflation-adjusted method allows considerably larger withdrawals. In the final year of your twenty-five years of retire-ment, the level income plan gives you the same $50,100, while the inflation-adjusted plan provides $92,662. Need I point out that the inflation-adjusted method is a much safer way to plan for retirement?

Throughout this book I have stressed the variability of returns and urged you to build a cushion to account for years in which your returns don't match the averages I used to build portfolios. Until recently there was no way to really effectively calculate the effects of variable returns on a portfolio over a long span of time. But increasingly the financial services industry is using a method called "Monte Carlo simulations" to project the effects of variable returns and other unpredictable events that might affect portfolio values over a long period of time. Since these simulations require quite a bit of computer power and time, they tend to be costly. If you're getting close to retirement, you might want to find a financial planner who uses the Monte Carlo technique to review your portfolio. The several hundred dollars it might cost will be well spent. If you want to try a simple version for free, visit the Web site www.financialengines.com, but be prepared to input considerable amounts of personal financial data for the engine to utilize.

INDEX